102 Useful
Excel 365 Functions

EXCEL 365 ESSENTIALS - BOOK 3

M.L. HUMPHREY

CONTENTS

CONTENTS (CONT.)

CONTENTS (CONT.)

CONTENTS (CONT.)

Introduction

Excel formulas and functions are essential to how I use Microsoft Excel. But I waited to cover them until the third book in the series, because you really can do a tremendous amount in Excel without using more than your basic math operators like the plus sign (+), minus sign (-), multiplication sign (*), and division sign (/).

Which you can do without really diving in on how formulas and functions work in Excel. But at some point it's a good idea to sit down and think through the difference between formulas and functions and to get a broader understanding of what functions Excel contains.

So that's what we're going to do here. I'm going to start with an introduction to how formulas and functions work in Excel, where you can find them, and some best practices for using them. And then we're going to dive in on actual functions.

It may seem strange to say this, but my goal in writing this book is to give you a book you can actually read cover-to-cover. I want it to be a resource, too, that you can come back to later when you need to know how to use X function. But for the first readthrough I have actually written this with a narrative flow from one function to the next.

So try to read it that way. And understand that if you don't read it that way there will be times when I say, "like we discussed with X function, Y function here also blah, blah, blah."

In this book I've chosen the most useful functions I know, like SUM for summing values, but I've also tried to present a wide sampling of the functions you can encounter in Excel.

And because I'm writing this for Excel 365 as it exists in December 2022, I've made a point of incorporating some of the newer functions that are available now in Excel but weren't previously, like XLOOKUP which is meant to replace VLOOKUP and HLOOKUP.

I'd say most users will probably only use about a dozen functions on a regular basis, but I can't tell from here which functions those will be for you. So I've tried to cover a broad enough range to give most users an insight into the functions they need and tried to cover enough functions in detail that even if I didn't cover your function here, I've given you the framework you need to work with that function.

In total, there are 102 functions covered in this book to some level of detail and another twelve that are mentioned in passing.

Sixty-eight of the functions have dedicated chapters. When functions work in a very similar way, like LEFT, RIGHT, and MID, they do share a chapter, but for each of those listed functions I give the function notation and definition at the start of the chapter. That chapter then includes a discussion of the functions as well as examples that apply them.

Often the chapter will include a screenshot showing sample data, the formula that was applied to that data, and the result.

(This is an upgrade from *50 Useful Excel Functions* and *50 More Excel Functions*, which were the original books I wrote on Excel formulas and functions. Those books were primarily text-based.)

After those detailed chapters, I cover an additional thirty-four functions in one chapter. That chapter quickly explains what each function does and often includes a brief example using the function, but there is no function notation and definition and no screenshot.

Finally, there are a dozen functions that I mention in passing, but that aren't specifically covered in this book. Functions like LEFTB which is a specific variation on LEFT that needs to be used for certain languages. Or functions like MODE and RANK that have been replaced by more specific functions in newer versions of Excel.

Another thing to know before we start is that I am not doing this alphabetically. Because I want this to be readable from cover to cover, I'm going to start by grounding you in some of the more simple or more useful functions and then we'll expand out from there.

If you don't want to read this book cover-to-cover I have listed the top seven functions I think you should know at the start of that section.

In the print version there is an index in the back that lists all of the functions in alphabetical order so that you can later come back and quickly find the function you need. (If you're reading in ebook you should be able to use the search function.)

While not every function I cover here will be useful to every reader of this book, at least be sure to read the generic introductory chapters because those really are applicable to any formulas and functions in Excel.

Also, I am covering Excel functions as they exist right now in Excel 365, but be aware that if someone has a fixed edition of Microsoft Excel, what Excel likes to call "on premise" versions, that they may not have all the same functions that you do. TEXTJOIN, XLOOKUP, and IFS, for example, are all great functions but also relatively new.

If you're working with outside parties who don't have Office 365, be very careful about using newer functions because they may not be able to use them in their version of Office. (I had this experience early in my consulting career. I found a great function, I think it was SUMIFS, that did all sorts of things I needed to do for my client. I used it to create a whole workbook for them, handed it off, and they couldn't use it because their version of Excel didn't include that function. Which meant I had to redo everything.)

So I'm going to act here like backwards compatibility is not an issue for you, but I'll drop a few comments to flag those functions that are new enough to be potential issues.

Okay then.

Let's get started with how formulas and functions work. But first I want to quickly review cell notation and how copying formulas works in Excel, things I touched upon in *Excel 365 for Beginners* but want to cover here again in case you didn't read that book.

Cell Notation and Copying Formulas

If you're going to work with formulas in Excel, then you need to understand how Excel references cells and what happens when you copy a formula to a different cell.

Cell Notation

Cells are referenced based upon their column and their row. By default, columns are lettered left to right, starting at A, and rows are numbered top to bottom, starting at 1.

(There is a setting to change the references so that both columns and rows are numbered, but we're not going to use that. It's R1C1 notation if you ever need it.)

So Cell A1 is the cell that is the intersection of Column A and Row 1. The top leftmost cell in a worksheet.

Cell B10 is the cell at the intersection of Column B and Row 10.

Cell BC25232 is the cell at the intersection of Column BC and Row 25232.

I write here Cell A1, but when you reference a cell in Excel, you just write it as A1.

If you want to reference more than one cell or cell range in a function then you can do so in a couple of ways.

To reference separate and discrete cells or cell ranges, you list each one and you separate them with a comma. So

A1,A2,A3

refers to Cells A1, A2, and A3.

When cells are touching you can instead reference them as a single range using the colon.

A1:A3

also refers to Cells A1, A2, and A3. Think of the colon as a "through".

You don't have to limit the use of the colon to a single row or column.

For example, you can use

A1:B25

to refer to all of the cells in Columns A and B and Rows 1 through 25.

To see what cells are covered for a range, start with the first cell (A1) and then go from there to the column listed for the second cell, (B), and then go down for all of those columns to the row listed for the second cell (25).

(When in doubt, you can input the cell reference in Excel and it will highlight your cells for you. Just type = and then the cell range into a cell and you'll see those cells surrounded by a colored border. The reverse is also true, you can start a formula with = and then go and select the cells you want to include, and Excel will write the cell notation for you.)

You can reference an entire column by using the letter and leaving off any numbers.

C:C

refers to all cells in Column C.

And you can do the same for a row by leaving off the letter.

10:10

refers to all the cells in Row 10.

This can be expanded to multiple columns (A:C) and multiple rows (5:9) by listing the starting column or row first and then using the colon and listing the ending column or row.

If you ever reference a cell in another worksheet or another workbook, this also needs to be addressed through cell notation.

For a cell in another worksheet, you put the sheet name as it appears on the worksheet tab followed by an exclamation point before the cell reference.

Sheet1!B1

is Cell B1 in the worksheet labeled Sheet 1.

For another workbook, put the name of the workbook in brackets before the worksheet name.

[Book1]Sheet2!$D$2

refers to Cell D2 in the worksheet labeled Sheet 2 in the workbook titled Book 1.

I should note here that I think it's a bad idea to reference data in another workbook due to the odds that the formula/function will break as soon as that other workbook is renamed or moved to a new location and so I generally don't do that.

Also, when it comes to cells in other worksheets (which I do use) or in other workbooks, I let Excel do the work for me. I start my formula and then I go and click on the cells I need from that other worksheet or workbook and let Excel figure out how to write that.

But I mention it because it is useful to know how this works in case you need to troubleshoot a bad result.

Copying or Cutting a Formula

To get the most use out of formulas in Excel, you need to understand how copying formulas in Excel works. That's because you can write a formula once, copy it, and paste it to thousands of cells, and Excel will automatically adjust that formula to its new location for you.

It's fantastic.

But the default for copying formulas is that every single cell reference in the formula adjusts for the new location of the formula.

Let me give you an example. One of the most basic Excel formulas adds two cells together. If I write:

$$=A1+B1$$

that is telling Excel to take the value in Cell A1 and add it to the value in Cell B1 and return that value in my current cell, let's say Cell C1.

You can see the formula displayed in the formula bar below as well as the value for that formula in Cell C1 in the worksheet:

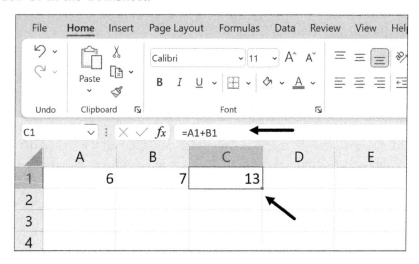

But what if instead of single entries like I have here, I have a hundred different values in Column A and a hundred different values in Column B and I want to add the values in Column A to the values in Column B for each row?

Excel makes this very easy to do, because if I take my formula in Cell C1 and I copy it down one row, Excel will automatically adjust that formula for me so that all of the cell references in the formula now reference cells that are also one row below.

For Cell C2 it will give me a formula of

$$=A2+B2$$

just by my clicking on Cell C1, copying (Ctrl + C), going to Cell C2, and pasting (Ctrl + V).

I can do this for a hundred rows at once by copying the formula in Cell C1 and then selecting a cell range (Cells C2 through C100) before I paste.

Excel will update every single one of those formulas based upon the relative position of the new location for the formula compared to where I copied it from.

In this situation, that's very easy to figure out.

If I copy from Row 1 to Row 50 and my formula was referencing Cells A1 and B1 it will now be referencing Cells A50 and B50.

But Excel does this for any cells in the entire worksheet. If I move over six columns and down three rows, it will adjust the column letter by six columns and the row number by three rows at the same time.

Which is great when that's what you want. But kind of horrible if you wanted something to stay fixed. Say I wanted to continue referring to Cells A1 and B1, I just wanted my formula in Cell H1 instead. Copy and paste is not going to work. Not without some tweaks.

If you have nothing else in that worksheet at the time, the easiest way to achieve that would be to insert columns to shift the values in Column C over to Column H, because the formula in Cell C1 will continue to reference those original cells even if you insert new columns or rows that move the formula.

But let's say you can't do that.

If you just need to move a formula to a new location but don't want any of the cell references to adjust, then you can cut and move the formula instead of copying it.

Click on the cell and use Ctrl + X and then go to the new location and use Ctrl + V. That moves the formula from its original location to the new one. If you want to keep the formula in its original location as well as move it, then click on the cell with the formula, go to the formula bar, highlight the formula there (Ctrl + A if you want the entire formula), copy it (Ctrl + C), hit Esc, go to the new cell, and then paste (Ctrl + V).

What about a situation where you're fine to copy the formula, but you want to make sure that it continues to reference either a specific cell or a specific row or column no matter where you copy that formula to?

Fortunately, Excel has a way to say "don't change this when you copy". The way you do that is to use the dollar sign ($) before the portion that you don't want to change.

If I write:

$$=\$A1+\$B1$$

And then I copy that formula from Column C to Column H, the A and B will not change. But because I didn't use a dollar sign in front of the row number, if I then copy that down the rows in Column H, the row values *will* change.

If you ever have a formula that's referencing a fixed value, like interest rate or currency conversion rate, and that location of that value will not change, then use a dollar sign before both the column and cell reference, like I have here to fix the reference to Cell A1:

$$=\$A\$1*B2$$

If you copy this formula down one row it will become:

$$=\$A\$1*B3$$

If you copy it over one row it will become:

$$=\$A\$1*C2$$

Another time when I find that I need to be careful about fixing cell references is when I'm copying a formula that references a cell range.

For example:

$$=A1/SUM(A1:A25)$$

is a simple formula for taking the total of the values in Cells A1 through A25 and then calculating what percent of that total is represented by the value in Cell A1.

Usually I want to take a formula like that and copy it down so that I'm doing the same calculation for the value in Cell A2 and in Cell A3 and so on. But if I don't lock the reference to Cells A1:A25 in the SUM portion of that formula, I end up with:

$$=A2/SUM(A2:A26)$$

That is not what I want. So I need to write the original formula as:

$$=A1/SUM(\$A\$1:\$A\$25)$$

That fixes the range that I'm summing so that all cells are divided by the same value when I copy that formula down.

(In this specific scenario I can check that the formula is working properly by taking the total of all of my calculations for Cells A1 through A25 because they should add up to 1 or 100%.)

Okay, so that was a brief overview of cell notation and copying and cutting formulas. Now let's talk about how formulas and functions work in Excel.

How Formulas and Functions Work

First, we need to define what formulas and functions are.

For purposes of this book, I'm going to define a formula in Excel as anything that is started with an equals sign and asks Excel to perform a calculation or task.

(Technically, you can start a formula with a plus or a minus sign as well, but Excel transforms those formulas into ones that use an equals sign anyway so we're just going to use an equals sign from here on out.)

I define a function as a command that is used within a formula to give instructions to Excel to perform a pre-defined task or set of tasks. In other words, a function is basically agreed-upon shorthand.

A formula in Excel could be as simple as:

$$=A1$$

Which is saying make the contents in this cell the same as the contents in Cell A1. It starts with an equals sign and is telling Excel to do something, so is a formula.

Usually, though, a formula is going to be more complex than that. Let's walk through a few examples.

Here is a simple formula that only uses the plus sign (+):

$$=A1+B1+C1$$

is telling Excel to sum the values in Cells A1, B1, and C1.

Here is that same calculation, but using a function (SUM) that when used tells Excel to sum the provided values:

$$=SUM(A1:C1)$$

(When I write a function in this book I will do so using capital letters like I just did with SUM.)

And here is that same calculation using a combination of a cell reference, the plus sign, and a function:

$$=A1+SUM(B1:C1)$$

Note here that even though I used a function (SUM), I didn't have to start the formula with that function. I did have to have something that connected my first part of the formula (A1) with the second part of the formula (SUM(B1:C1)). In this case, the plus sign (+).

All four of the examples above are formulas, but only two of them incorporated a function. You will see a large number of examples as we work our way through the rest of this book, some much more complex than these, including ones that use multiple functions either side-by-side in the same formula or "nested" where one function is wrapped around another in the formula.

In the example above I was able to write a formula using the plus sign that performed the same task as the SUM function, but the reason functions exist is for those situations where manually writing that formula becomes impossible.

I might be able to manually write the equivalent of:

$$=SUM(A1:A100)$$

which sums the values in Cells A1 through A100.

But there's no way I'd ever want to manually write the equivalent of:

$$=SUM(A:A)$$

which sums the values of in all cells in Column A. That could be over a million values. Even if Excel let me write that, I doubt I could do so without making an error.

Okay. A few more things to know about functions.

All functions require the use of parens. You write the function name, the next thing you include is that opening paren, then you tell Excel the information it needs to perform that function (which will vary by function), and then you end with a closing paren.

Some functions have no inputs, but they still require parens. For example:

$$=TODAY( )$$

is a formula that will return today's date using the TODAY function. It doesn't need additional inputs, but it does still require both an opening and closing paren.

(Sidenote: The RAND function also does not require inputs but when I tried to use it here as an example, Word turned it into a random selection of text. Fun times!)

There's far more complexity to working with formulas and functions that we'll cover in the rest of this book via example.

For now, to sum up. The basic rules of building a formula are (1) start with an equals sign, (2) if you use a function follow that immediately with an opening paren, (3) for any function you use provide all of the required inputs, (4) for any function, close that function out with a closing paren after you've provided the required inputs, and (5) if you use multiple calculations, value ranges, or functions in a formula they must be connected to one another via something like a plus sign (+), minus sign (-), comma(,) etc. What needs to be used will depend upon where in the formula it's used.

We will demonstrate all of these rules many, many times throughout this book, so don't worry if they don't make perfect sense right now. This is more to have as a reference if you ever get stuck with a formula that isn't working for you.

Okay. Next up, how to see a formula in Excel.

How To See a Formula

Once you've entered a formula in a cell and leave that cell, the result of the formula is what will display in that cell in your worksheet by default.

You can go back to that cell and look at the formula bar to see the formula. Here I've clicked on Cell C1 which contains the formula =A1+B1:

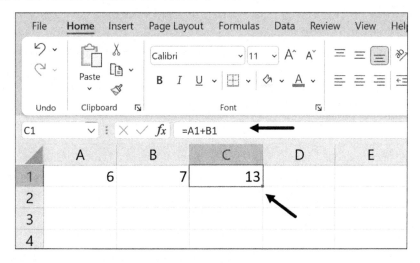

You can see the result of the formula in Cell C1 and the formula in the formula bar.

If you double-click on a cell that contains a formula, the cell will also display the formula and Excel will highlight any cells used in that formula and color-code the elements of the formula and the cells to match. Like so:

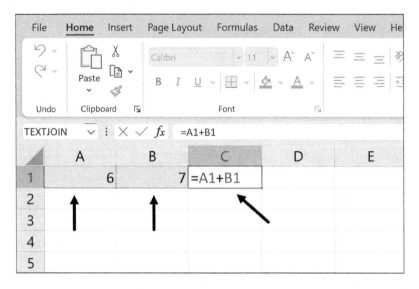

It's a little hard to see in print, but Cells A1 and B1 are now highlighted in different colors and those colors match the color shown for their cell references in the formula in Cell C1.

This makes it easy to see which cell is being used in which part of a formula, which becomes especially helpful when dealing with very complex formulas.

If you double-click on a cell to see the formula in the cell, you can exit the cell using Esc, Enter, tab or by clicking away.

When you exit a cell with a formula, the cell will return to showing the calculated value.

Another way to see that color coding of the cells used in a formula is to click on the cell you want and then click into the formula bar like I have here:

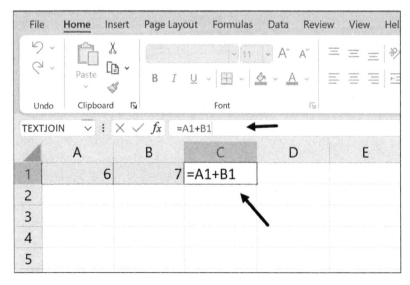

Now the cell and the formula bar both show the formula and the cells that are used in the formula are color-coded, but the cursor is in the formula bar.

No matter what you do, the formula bar will always contain the formula. But there may be times when you want to see the formula in the main workspace for multiple cells at once.

I do not need this often, but it can be a quick way to make sure that your formulas are all working properly. Here, for example, I have written a formula in Column P that is meant to take the values in Column N and convert them from GBP (the currency in the UK) to USD (the currency in the United States):

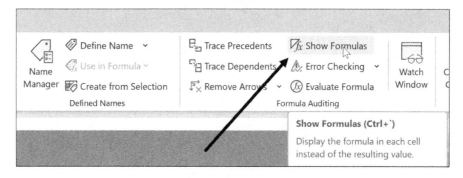

You can see the formula for Cell P16 in the screenshot:

$$=ROUND(N16*1.21,2)$$

1.21 is the conversion rate on that day to turn a value in GBP into a value in USD. I'm using the ROUND function here so that we are still dealing with dollars and cents after the calculation is done. If I didn't use the ROUND function, I'd end up with results like 3.2912.

Since 1 GBP is the same as \$1.21 USD, the values in Column P should be greater than the values in Column N.

But if you look closely at the other results in Column P, some of those values are not greater than the values in Column N. In the third row of values (technically Row 54, because I have this data filtered to just GBP results) the values in Columns N and P are the same.

So the formula in that row is off. Same for the next two rows.

To see the difference between our formulas in those cells, we can go to the Formula Auditing section of the Formulas tab and click on Show Formulas.

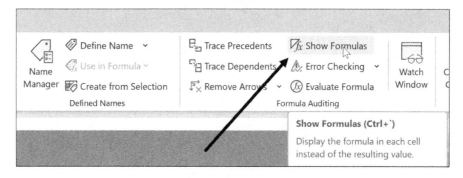

That will take any cell that uses a formula and instead of showing the result of the formula it will display the actual formula. Like so:

N	O	P
Royalty ▾	**Currency** ▾	⍓ **Convert to USD**
2.72	GBP	➤ =ROUND(N16*1.21,2)
0	GBP	=ROUND(N34*1.21,2)
1.96	GBP	➤ =ROUND(N54,2)
6.13	GBP	=ROUND(N60,2)
2.76	GBP	=ROUND(N73,2)
2.76	GBP	=ROUND(N80*1.21,2)
0.35	GBP	=ROUND(N81*1.21,2)
2.46	GBP	=ROUND(N82*1.21,2)
2.76	GBP	=ROUND(N89*1.21,2)
2.76	GBP	=ROUND(N101*1.21,2)
2.46	GBP	=ROUND(N107*1.21,2)
2.76	GBP	=ROUND(N112*1.21,2)
2.76	GBP	=ROUND(N118*1.21,2)

We can then quickly see that there is a difference between the formula used in those top two rows and the formula used in the next three rows.

We should expect our formula to adjust the cell references as we copy it down, like it did in the second row, but what happens in that third row is that we lose part of the formula. The *1.21 portion of the formula is missing.

Showing the formulas lets us quickly see that issue and also see that it's an issue across three rows. I can fix it by copying the formula from Cell P16 down to those three cells.

I do not keep my worksheets set to display formulas like this because it keeps me from seeing my calculation results.

Also, you'll notice that it changed the formatting of my column widths when I changed that view. I don't personally like that, so it's another reason to keep this turned off unless needed.

To turn it off, just click on Show Formulas again.

Okay. Now let's discuss the most basic type of formula, one that just uses mathematical notation to perform calculations such as addition, subtraction, multiplication, and division.

Basic Math Calculations

I did already cover this in *Excel 365 for Beginners*, but I wanted to cover it again for those who didn't read that book, because a large part of the calculations you do in Excel will likely just involve simple math like addition, subtraction, division, and multiplication.

Which means it's important to know these mathematical functions. So let's run through them real quick.

Addition

Addition uses the plus (+) sign.

If I want to add 2 and 3, I can write:

$$=2+3$$

If those values are already stored in other cells, let's say Cells A1 and B1, I can instead write:

$$=A1+B1$$

If I want to add 2, 3, and 4, I can write:

$$=2+3+4$$

And if those values are already stored in Cells A1, B1, and C1, I can instead write:

$$=A1+B1+C1$$

Subtraction

To subtract one number from another you use the minus (-) sign. With subtraction order matters. Two minus three is not the same as three minus two.

If I want to subtract 2 from 3, I can write:

$$=3-2$$

If those values are already stored in other cells, let's say 3 is in Cell A1 and 2 is in Cell B1, I can instead write:

$$=A1-B1$$

If I want to subtract 2 and 3 from 6, I can write:

$$=6-2-3$$

And if those values are already stored in Cells with 6 in A1, 2 in B1, and 3 in C1, I can instead write:

$$=A1-B1-C1$$

Multiplication

To multiply two numbers you use the asterisk (*) sign.
    If I want to multiply 2 times 3, I can write:

$$=2*3$$

If those values are already stored in other cells, let's say Cells A1 and B1, I can instead write:

$$=A1*B1$$

If I want to multiply 2, 3, and 4, I can write:

$$=2*3*4$$

And if those values are already stored in Cells A1, B1, and C1, I can instead write:

$$=A1*B1*C1$$

Division

To divide two numbers you use the forward slash (/) between them. As with subtraction, order matters. Two divided by three is not the same as three divided by two.
    If I want to divide 2 by 3, I can write:

$$=2/3$$

If those values are already stored in other cells, let's say 3 is in Cell A1 and 2 is in Cell B1,

I can instead write:

$$=B1/A1$$

Other Math Operators

Those are the most common math operators in Excel, but you can also use others such as the caret ($\wedge$) symbol to indicate taking a value to a power. So:

$$=2\wedge3$$

would be 2 cubed or 2 times 2 times 2. And:

$$=4\wedge.5$$

would take the square root of 4. Also,

$$=27\wedge(1/3)$$

would take the cube root of 27.

$$* * *$$

In that last example, by putting 1/3 in parens I told Excel to make that calculation first before taking the root of 27.

By default, calculations are performed left to right and certain operations are performed first.

But you can use parens to change this. There is a help document titled "Calculation operators and precedence in Excel" which you can find through the Help tab in Excel by searching for "order of precedence" that will walk through that in much more detail.

It lists the order in which calculations are done by Excel and also lists a number of additional operators (such as > for greater than) that are useful to know when working with formulas and functions in Excel. We'll cover more of this later as it comes up in relation to certain functions.

Also, for addition and multiplication there are functions you can use as well (SUM and PRODUCT), which we will cover soon.

Where To Find Functions

Now let's talk about functions in more detail. The first thing you need to know is where to find functions in Excel.

We're going to discuss over a hundred Excel functions in this book, but there are far, far more functions than that in Excel, and chances are at some point you'll need one I didn't cover here.

To find the functions available in Excel, you can go to the Formulas tab. There is a section called Function Library that lists various categories of functions.

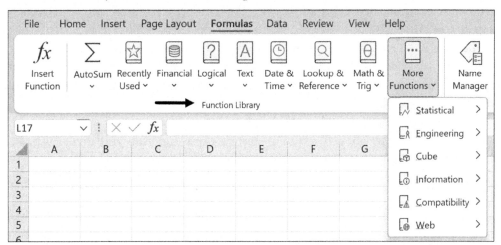

Mine shows Recently Used, Financial, Logical, Text, Date & Time, Lookup & Reference, Math & Trig, and then there's a dropdown for More Functions that shows the categories Statistical, Engineering, Cube, Information, Compatibility, and Web.

Click on the dropdown arrow next to any of the categories and you'll see an alphabetical listing of functions that fall under that heading, like I've done here for Math & Trig:

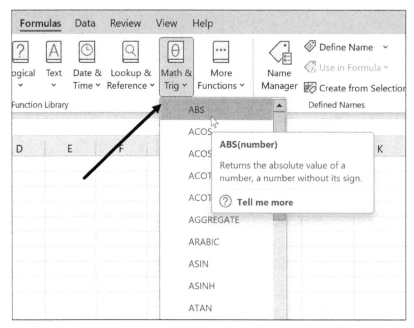

Now, unless you know what you're looking for, this listing probably won't help you much because the functions are named things like ASIN, ATAN, etc.

You can hold your cursor over each of the names and Excel will provide a brief description of the function for you, like I did above with ABS, but for some of the lists that's a lot of functions to look through.

Each description also includes a Tell Me More at the end of the description.

If you click on that option, the Help task pane will open to the Excel Functions (By Category) tab. You can then find the function you're interested in and click on its name to open the function-specific help.

I use a different method to find the functions I need.

What I do is click into my cell where I want to use a function and then I use the Insert Function option available on the far left-hand side of the Formulas tab.

This brings up the Insert Function dialogue box, which you can see in the screenshot below.

In the top section under where it says "Search for a function" you can type what you're looking to do and then click on Go. (Be sure that the category dropdown right below the search box is set to All unless you know for sure what category your function falls under.)

Excel will provide a list of functions that it thinks meet your search criteria. Sometimes this list is very far off, so don't just accept the first choice blindly.

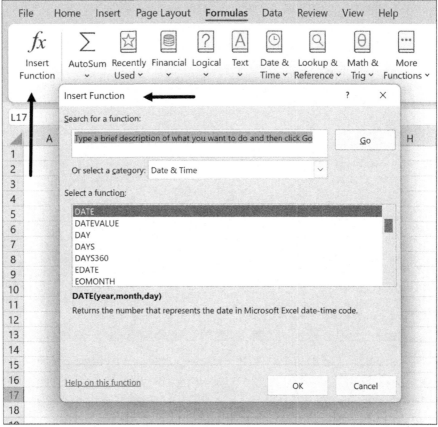

You can left-click on each of the listed functions to see a brief description of the function directly below the box where the functions are listed.

You will also see in the description for each function a list of the required inputs for that function as well.

For DATE, which is the selected function in the screenshot above, you can see that it "Returns the number that represents the date in Microsoft Excel date-time code" and that the inputs are a year, month, and day value.

(We'll cover how dates in Excel work later.)

For the sixty-plus functions in this book that have dedicated chapters, I will list the description and the inputs for each function.

If you need more information on a function than you see in the dialogue box, you can click on the "Help on this function" link in the bottom left corner of the dialogue box. That will bring up a website specific to that function. For any new-to-you function I recommend always at least skimming the help text. There can be some interesting quirks in how Excel functions work that are not obvious or intuitive.

Otherwise, you can just click on the function you want and choose OK.

This will insert the function into whichever cell you were clicked into before you chose Insert Function. You will also see a Function Arguments dialogue box that lists the inputs your function needs and provides a location for you to input those values so that Excel can build your formula for you.

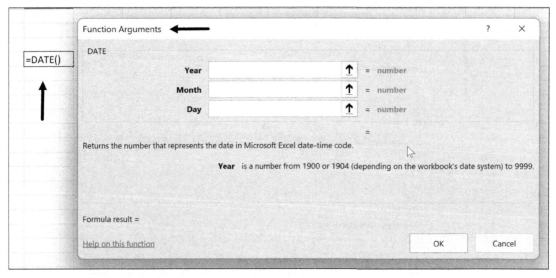

You can use the dialogue box if it helps. It allows you to input either numeric values or use cell references by clicking in each of those white input fields and then typing or selecting the cells in your worksheet. As you do so, Excel will show a sample result in the bottom corner of the dialogue box where it says "Formula Result =".

If you don't want to use the dialogue box, which I usually don't, you can close it by clicking on OK and then OK on the error dialogue box that will appear when you do that.

This will let you type in the values directly into the formula bar or cell that you want to use, which will now contain the function name minus its required inputs.

So =DATE() as an example.

(If you X out that dialogue box instead of using OK, the function name will also go away.)

If you used the dialogue box, when you're done, click OK and the calculated value will appear in your cell. Otherwise, add your inputs for your function directly in the cell/formula bar and then hit Enter. If you did it right, you'll see your value. If you did it wrong, you'll get an error message. (See the chapter on When Things Go Wrong for help on how to fix common error messages.)

* * *

You can always go back to a cell and edit the formula either through the formula bar or by double-clicking on the cell to make the formula appear.

* * *

If you already know the function you want to use but aren't sure about the required inputs, start typing a formula with the function name into your worksheet, like I've done here for SUM:

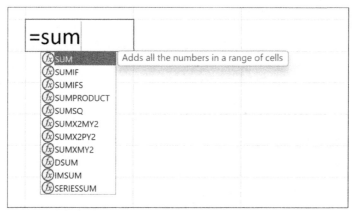

Excel will list all functions that include the text you've typed and will show you the description of what each one does as you click through that list.

Double-click on the one you want from the list and Excel will change your text to that function and include the opening paren. Or, if you have the function name you want already typed into the cell, just use your opening paren to start providing your inputs.

When you type that opening paren, Excel will switch over to showing the inputs required for that function.

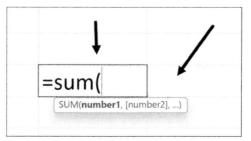

Here you can see that for the SUM function it wants a number or series of numbers. (When it says number that can also be a cell reference or cell range reference. We'll cover examples in the chapter on SUM.)

If you click on the function name in the pop-up box below the cell after you've typed the opening paren, Excel will open the Excel Help task pane on the right-hand side of the screen that is specific to that function.

(Which is why if I need help with a function I prefer to start my formula and then click on the function name to open the help task pane. It's the best way to get help without opening an annoying pop-up website or having to navigate to the help page I need.)

* * *

If none of that works to help you find the function you need, then an Internet search is probably your best option. A quick search for something like "How do I get Excel to identify the day of the week from a date?" will usually get you the function name you need to use. (Answer: The TEXT function.)

When Things Go Wrong

In the earlier versions of this book I had this section at the end after I discussed all of the functions. But as you're working your way through this book you will probably encounter some of these errors, so I decided to move it to the front. Consider this chapter a reference chapter for now that you can come back to if you're experimenting in your own worksheet and something doesn't work.

Also, I've tried to cover all of the error types you may see, but it's possible I missed something obscure, so if you ever get stuck either use Excel's help or email me.

#REF!

If you see #REF! in a cell it's probably because you deleted a value that that cell was referencing in a formula.

So if you have =A1+B1+C1+D1 in a cell and then you delete Column C that would create a #REF! error. Excel won't adjust the formula and drop the missing value, it will return this error message instead.

To see where the cell generating the error was in your formula, double-click in the cell with the #REF! message or click on the cell and look to the formula bar.

This is what I see when I delete Column C after writing the above formula in what was Column E:

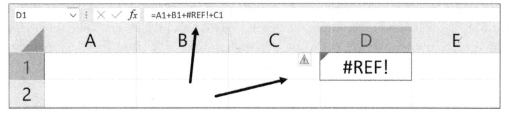

That says:

$$=A1+B1+\#REF!+C1$$

It's a little tricky with something like this formula to know what's missing. We know that there was a cell reference of some sort in the third position that is now gone, but it's not clear what was there. And note how what was D1 changed to C1 because I deleted the original Column C and Excel changed the cell references dynamically to account for that.

When this happens, if you don't think you needed that particular portion of that formula, just delete it from the formula. If you know what should go there and it still exists elsewhere, click into the cell and replace the #REF! with the correct cell reference.

Or, if this occurred because you deleted supporting data (usually my issue), then Undo, and either leave everything alone or copy your results and paste special-values so that your formulas are converted into static results that are no longer impacted by changes in their source data.

#VALUE!

According to Excel, a #VALUE! error means you typed your formula wrong or you're referencing a cell that's the wrong type of cell.

If you're using dates, see if the date is left-aligned. If it is, then chances are Excel is treating that date as a text entry not a date entry. That means, for example, that subtraction won't work on it.

Same with numbers. If you use SUM and get this error, make sure that your numbers are formatted as numbers and not text. (This shouldn't be a common problem, but could be if you've imported a data file from elsewhere.)

Or it can mean that you're referencing a data source that is no longer available, like another workbook that was moved or renamed. (Hence why I try to avoid referencing external workbooks. I tend to try to "tidy up" and move things around when a project is over and then I run into something like this.)

#DIV/0!

This is a common error to see when you've written a formula that requires division. If I input the formula =A1/B1 and there are no values in Cells A1 and B1, Excel will return #DIV/0!

You need a numeric value for your denominator to stop this from happening. (The numerator can be blank, but not the denominator.)

I often use an IF or IFS function to suppress the #DIV/0! error when I have a data table where values haven't been input yet. You can also use the IFERROR function to do this. We'll cover all three functions in detail later.

#N/A

According to Excel, an #N/A error means that Excel isn't finding what it was asked to look for. In other words, there's no solution.

This occurs most often with functions like XLOOKUP, VLOOKUP, HLOOKUP, MATCH, etc. when you tell Excel to look for a specific value and it can't find it.

This can be valuable information that perhaps points to a weakness in your data or your function. For example, it could indicate that the data in your lookup table is in a different format from the data in your analysis table. Or that there are extra spaces in the entries in one or the other table. Or that you chose the wrong type of match to look for.

But if you know this is going to happen and don't want to see the #N/A in your results, you can use the IFNA function to suppress that result and replace it with a zero, a blank space, or even text.

#NUM!

According to Excel, you will see this error when there are numeric values in a formula or function that aren't valid.

The example Excel gives involves using $1,000 in a formula instead of 1000, but when I just tried this to validate it, Excel wouldn't even allow me to use that formula. It wanted to fix the formula for me as soon as I hit Enter. So this may be more of an issue in older versions of Excel.

Excel will also return this error message if an iterative function can't find a result or if the result that would be returned by the formula is too large or too small. (If you're running into this error for those reasons chances are you're doing some pretty advanced things, so we're not going to worry about that here other than to let you know that's the issue to look for.)

#SPILL!

In newer versions of Excel you will get a #SPILL! error when using a function that can return more than one value where there is not enough room for Excel to return all of the results. The way to fix this is to clear those cells that have content that are preventing Excel from providing its results or to move the formula that uses that function somewhere it has room to return all of its results.

#NAME?

I usually see this error message when I start to write a formula in a cell that uses a function and then hit enter before I've provided my inputs. So if I type =RANK and then enter, Excel gives me this error.

That's because you can name cell ranges in Excel, so when I do that Excel looks for a named range called "RANK". Since one doesn't exist, it generates an error.

Usually my fix for this error is to delete the half-finished formula I started or to finish it. But if you actually are working with named ranges then double-check your name.

Circular References

Excel will also flag for you any time that you write a formula that references itself. (I do this on occasion without meaning to.)

For example, if in Cell A5 you type =SUM(A1:A5), Excel will display a dialogue box when you hit Enter that says, in part, "There are one or more circular references where a formula refers to its own cell either directly or indirectly."

Say OK and then go back to the cell with the formula and fix the issue. Help will open a website that describes the error.

I usually know what I did when I get this error message, but sometimes a circular reference error can be generated by an indirect reference. Meaning you're referencing a cell that's referencing another cell and it's that other cell that's driving the issue.

If you can't figure out the cause and Excel doesn't "helpfully" start drawing connections on your worksheet to show it to you, click on the cell with the problematic formula and then go to the Formulas tab and under Formula Auditing click on Trace Precedents to see what values are feeding that cell.

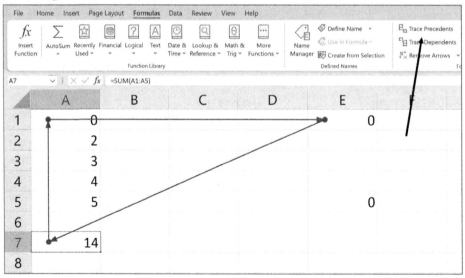

Above I have a formula in Cell A7 that is taking the sum of the values in Cells A1 through A5. But the value in Cell A1 is taken from Cell E1. Cell E1 is equal to 30 divided by the value in

Cell A7. That means Cell A7 is trying to add a value from Cell A1 that includes Cell A7 in its calculation, which isn't possible.

The blue arrows that Excel has drawn between Cells A1, E1, and A7 tell us that the circular reference involves one of those cells.

Too Few Arguments

I also on occasion will try to use a function and get a warning message that I've used too few arguments for the function.

When that happens, check that you've included enough inputs for the function to work. Anything listed that isn't in brackets is required. So =RANDBETWEEN(bottom, top) requires that you enter values for both bottom and top but =CONCATENATE(text1, [text2],…) only requires one input.

If you don't have an input for every required item, then that's the issue and it can be fixed by providing the missing item. I sometimes, for example, try to write =ROUND(1.234) without including the second part of the ROUND function that tells Excel how many decimal places to round to.

Also make sure that each of your inputs are properly separated by commas and that any quotation marks or parens in a complex or nested function are in the right place. I will often see this error because I'm missing a comma or paren somewhere in a complex formula.

General Wonkiness

Sometimes everything seems fine but the formula just doesn't seem to be giving the right answer. If it's a complex formula, break it down into its components and make sure that each component works on a standalone basis. If they do, then check your parens, quotes, brackets, etc. that are meant to separate the different components and set their order.

Also, as mentioned above, you can double-click on a cell that contains a formula and Excel will color code each of the separate components that are feeding that formula and also highlight the related cells in a matching color in your worksheet.

Confirm that the highlighted cells are the correct ones to use in the formula. Sometimes you can get an issue like this because you copied a formula to new cells without locking a cell reference or cell range that's used in the formula.

Also, sometimes there are choices you can make with a function that impact the result, like whether you remembered to sort the value range before using VLOOKUP.

If you're working with a function you're not familiar with, open the Excel Help for the function and read through it. That will often give a list of common issues encountered with that particular function.

A Warning and Best Practices

Before we start our discussion of the actual functions, which will be the bulk of this book, I want to provide a warning and some best practices I've found helpful when working with formulas in Excel.

The Warning

There is a saying, "garbage in, garbage out" which absolutely applies to working in Excel. Excel is not a person, it is not sentient. (Yet. Haha.) All it is is a series of instructions that you trigger with what you input into your worksheet.

For example, you go to a cell and type something. The instructions are to keep what you typed and display it back to you.

With formulas and functions, using that equals sign is an instruction. It says, "Hey, I need you to calculate something or perform a task for me." And then you tell it exactly what to calculate or do and what information to use for that.

But at the end of the day what it does and how it does that is driven by you. So never ever trust blindly. If you look at a result and think, "Hmmm. I'm not sure that makes sense," then you need to go back and check what you told Excel to do and what information you told it to use.

Are your cell ranges correct? Did you fix cell references that should be fixed? Did you not fix cell references when they should adjust? Is that the right formula? Or function? Are the parens in the right places so that the right things are being done in the right order? Is your data formatted correctly if that matters for that formula?

All of that can impact what Excel does. It's a really helpful tool, but that's all it is and it's down to you, the user, to use it properly. If you don't, you'll get garbage. So I always encourage understanding what you're trying to do and how things should look before you actually rely on Excel to do whatever it is for you.

Which is where some of these best practices come from. Let's discuss those now.

Best Practices

Make Your Assumptions Visible

You can easily build a formula where all of the information to make the calculation is contained within that one cell and largely invisible to anyone working in that worksheet.

So if I want to add the values 10, 20, and 30 together I can do that in one cell using =10+20+30 and all anyone will see in the worksheet is the result of that calculation, 60.

You may be tempted to do this because it's clean. All that people see is what you want them to, the result of your calculation.

And maybe you don't expect to have to adjust those values, so you don't see an issue in having your formula built that way.

But I would encourage you not to do this.

In my experience, a best practice in terms of building formulas is to have any fixed values or assumptions visible somewhere in your workbook. The reason to do this is so that someone can easily see the assumptions that fed the calculation.

For example, let's say you're calculating how much you'll make if you sell your house. You figure you'll have to spend $2,500 to clean the place up a bit, pay a commission of 5%, and that the house is currently worth $500,000.

Now, if you sat down to discuss this with your spouse you could just show them the results of that calculation *or* you could show them the assumptions you made and what result that gave you.

Showing the assumptions means that if your spouse knows that they have a realtor friend who will charge 3% instead of 5%, they can give you that feedback. Or they can tell you that they think you should also repaint and fix that front step and rent a storage unit to clear out some junk and that the $2,500 you think is needed for clean-up seems low.

Without showing them your assumptions, they aren't going to be able to provide that input.

Also, even if it's just for you, if you bury your assumptions in your calculation field they're easy to forget about. Which can be dangerous if they're wrong or circumstances change. Or, and I've done this, you come back six months later and there are six values in your formula and you have to waste five minutes trying to figure out what each value stands for. Was that 5% the realtor fee? Or was that the clean-up cost? Or the moving cost? Who knows.

So, make assumptions visible. Save yourself some headache, and the risk that you don't know there's an assumed value in your calculation.

Use Paste Special - Values

The other thing I do that you may or may not want to do depending on why you're using Excel is that I frequently use Paste Special – Values when I'm done with performing a set of calculations.

Do not do this if the calculations you performed need to be updated on an ongoing basis.

But I do a lot of calculations where I want to keep the results for reference but will not be recalculating any values, and I want to lock those values down so that I don't lose them or inadvertently recalculate them by changing a value in an input cell or deleting data that fed those calculations.

(Deleting data I used in a calculation to tidy things up and turning my calculation fields into error messages is something I do far too often.)

The simple way to do this is to select the cells, use Ctrl + C to copy, and then right-click and under Paste Options choose the Values option (the one with the 123 on the clipboard). This will replace any calculated cells in that range with just the values of the calculation.

You basically just paste the results from the formulas right on top of the cells that contained those formulas.

After you do that, instead of a formula, for example, =A1+B1, you'll have a cell that just contains the result of having added Cells A1 and B1 together. That means if you then delete the values in Cells A1 and B1 it won't change the cell with the result in it.

Don't Mess With Your Raw Data

To the extent possible, you should always store your raw data in one location and do all of your calculations and manipulations on that data elsewhere or on a copy of that data.

(Ideally you would also record all of the steps you followed to take that raw data and turn it into your final product, but it's not as easy to do in something like Excel as it is in a programming language like R where you are basically writing a script of steps to follow.)

If you don't keep your raw data untouched, all it takes is one bad sort or one bad function and your data can be irreparably changed in a way you can't fix. Usually you can undo if you notice it immediately, but chances are you won't.

If, on the other hand, you keep your raw data separate, there is nothing you can't come back from. You might have to redo all of your work, but you won't be left with a data set that's useless.

I will also save versions of my worksheets when I'm working on something particularly complicated. That way I can go back to a stage where everything was working without having to start over from scratch. Just be sure to label your files clearly so that you know which is the most recent version.

If naming your files with the date I suggest using YYYYMMDD as the date format because then the files will sort in order. So, Important File 20220101, Important File 20220305, and Important File 20220802 will let those files sort in most recent to least recent order without a hitch.

If I have two files on the same day I add v1, v2, etc.

Test Your Formulas

If I'm going to apply a formula to a large range of data I will usually test that formula on a much smaller sample of my data where I can visually or manually evaluate the results.

So if I'm writing a formula to sum customer transactions for customers from Alaska who bought Widgets (using SUMIFS), I'll run that formula against just ten rows of data to make sure that it's doing what I think it should before I apply it to ten thousand rows of data.

As much as possible you should always either check your formulas on a subset of data or "gut check" your results.

Don't just accept the value Excel gives you without questioning whether it actually makes sense.

Be especially wary when it comes to edge cases. If the formula is supposed to calculate for values equal to or greater than 25, then you need to test 24.99, 25, and 25.01 to make sure that they all work properly.

(I personally have a bad habit of saying it applies for 25 or greater and then writing the formula as greater than 25.)

So, test, test, test. And then check, check, check.

Also, if you're building a really complex formula it's a good idea to test it as you go to make sure that all of the components are working properly and that the end result is the expected result.

So I will build each component separately before combining them all in one cell and make sure that the ultimate result of that single formula matches the result I get when I go step-by-step.

But also check to see if there's a function that already does what you want. Especially when dealing with common calculations, there just might be. For example, SUMPRODUCT is a way to combine multiplication and addition that can save a lot of time. (We'll cover it in a moment.)

Consider Compatibility Issues

If you are designing a workbook that will be used by anyone other than you, consider what their circumstances are and what that means for the format and functions you can use. Some functions did not exist in early versions of Excel. Some functionality also did not exist. Even some colors did not exist.

When it's just you, you can use Excel as it exists in front of you with no issues. In thirty years of using Office products it has been very rare that they take something away. I won't swear they won't, because there are always new developers coming up who don't understand their user base and think "desktops are stupid" or something similar, but generally going forward in Excel you will have access to what you have right now.

But Excel does improve over time. And if you're going to share your creation with someone who has an older version of Excel they may not be able to do what you can.

So if you're going to share Excel files with people outside your organization be very careful what functions you use to create whatever you're going to share. Make sure they're backwards compatible as much as you possibly can. Also keep an eye on number of rows/columns used and filtering.

In some cases you may even need to share the file as a different file type. I think we're about at the end of needing to save files as .xls files instead of .xlsx files for backwards compatibility, but maybe not quite yet. And the new free Office online options may help with a lot of this, but better to not get that email or phone call that says, "I can't open this" or "This doesn't work."

Excel Function Notation

I have mentioned this briefly a few times now, but before we start working our way through individual functions, I wanted to cover it again.

Excel provides for every function a description of what the function does and a list of the required inputs and the order they need to be provided in. In the detail chapters that follow, I have provided this information at the top of each chapter for the functions covered in that chapter.

Here I want to discuss what you're seeing when you see that. This is the function notation for SUM:

$$SUM(number1, [number2],...)$$

If an input is listed in brackets, like number2 is above, then that input is not required. So the SUM function can have just one input, number1.

If there is a ... at the end of the list of inputs that tells you that you can have more than just those two inputs.

If you go to the help for a function it will tell you how many inputs are allowed. SUM allows up to 255 values separated by commas.

But it's also important to note here that the number1 doesn't mean a fixed value like 5. It can be a cell reference. So I can write:

$$=SUM(M:O)$$

which will sum all of the cells in Columns M, N, and O, which is over 3 million potential values but in cell notation is equivalent to SUM(number1) where number1 is M:O.

Also, some functions work in multiple ways so they require that you choose TRUE or FALSE as an input to tell them how to perform.

For example, the TEXTJOIN function has the following inputs:

$$TEXTJOIN(delimiter, ignore\_empty, text1, [text2],...)$$

That second input "ignore_empty" is a TRUE/FALSE condition asking if a cell is blank do you ignore what's in that cell or do you include a blank space.

When dealing with a TRUE/FALSE input there are multiple ways to write that. You can skip putting any value if you are okay with the default way the function works, you can type TRUE or FALSE, or you can type 1 or 0.

Also, note here that TEXTJOIN includes three distinct mandatory inputs. For all functions, the inputs must be provided in that listed order for the function to work. For TEXTJOIN the required first input is the delimiter, for example.

Finally, for some functions there are specific values for an input that provide specific results. See CONVERT for an example of this. You'll generally see a list of those choices as you type your formula and reach the point where you're asked to provide that input for that function.

We'll cover a number of them in this book as well so stay with me and you'll understand how that all works by the time we're done.

Okay. Now we're ready to dive in on specific functions. Let's go. Fun times ahead.

Top Functions To Know

For the impatient among you, this is the list to use if you don't want to read this book cover to cover. At least read about the ones I list here so you can pick up some valuable tools and get a feel for how robust Excel is.

Top functions to know:

1. SUM – sums a range of specified values

2. IFS – returns one value if a specified condition is met, but another value if it is not

3. SUMIFS – sums values only if the specified conditions are met

4. TEXTJOIN – joins text that's stored in separate cells into one entry

5. XLOOKUP – looks up a value in a table based on a search criteria

6. ROUND – rounds a number to a specified number of decimal places

7. CONVERT – converts a value from one measurement to another

Master these seven and the math operators and you'll have a good solid foundation to work from. But if you're okay with going on a longer journey, then turn the page and let's start with one of the most useful functions in Excel, SUM.

The SUM Function

Notation:
SUM(number1, [number2],…)

Excel Definition:
Adds all the numbers in a range of cells.

The SUM function is probably the most basic function in Excel and I'd suspect also the most widely used.

What the SUM function does is add numbers together. These can be numbers that you type directly into the function (not recommended) or they can be values that are stored in other cells.

Cells do not need to be touching for their values to be added together, although it's much easier to write your SUM function if they are.

To use the function you must include at least one number (or cell range) within the parens. Some examples of formulas that use the SUM function are:

=SUM(2,3,4)

which adds the numbers 2, 3, and 4 together. And:

=SUM(A1,A2,A3)

which adds the values in Cells A1, A2, and A3 together.

But those aren't the best ways to use the SUM function, because they still require listing each individual value. Where the true power of SUM comes into play is when it's used with cell ranges.

Like here where we're telling Excel to sum all of the values in Column A:

=SUM(A:A)

Or here where it's being told to sum all of the values in Row 5:

$$=SUM(5:5)$$

Or here where it's summing all of the values in Columns A through H:

$$=SUM(A:H)$$

As I mentioned above, you don't have to sum values that are next to one another. So here, we're summing two value ranges, the values in Cells A1 through A3 as well as the values in Cells B2 through B6:

$$=SUM(A1:A3,B2:B6)$$

* * *

Pretty simple, right? SUM, opening paren, whatever you want to add together using cell notation, closing paren. Done.

As mentioned in the introductory section, the formula you write doesn't have to start with SUM.

You can also combine SUM with a minus sign to back into a formula for subtracting a large number of values.

Say, for example, I have a value in Cell B1 and I want to subtract from that value any values in Column A. I can write:

$$=B1-SUM(A:A)$$

Or if I wanted to subtract the values in Column C from the value in Cell A1 but then also add the values in Column E, I could do that as well:

$$=A1-SUM(C:C)+SUM(E:E)$$

Note as we discussed before that the only place you need an equals sign is at the start of a formula. Otherwise, you just use the function name when you need it.

* * *

One more note. Sometimes you can get Excel to build your SUM function for you using AutoSum.

If you have a range of values and you want to take the sum of those values, click into the cell at the end of that range (row or column), and then click on the AutoSum option in the Editing section of the Home tab.

Excel will, by default, insert a SUM function into that cell with a specified range that covers all continuous cells from that point.

This is best demonstrated with an example. Below, I have clicked into Cell A11 and used AutoSum.

	A	B	C	D	E
1	2				
2	3				
3	4				
4	5		**AutoSum**		
5	6		**Used**		
6					
7	3				
8	4				
9	5				
10	6				
11	=SUM(A7:A10)				
12	SUM(**number1**, [number2], ...)				
13					

You can see that the SUM function Excel inserted for me summed the values in Cells A7 through A10, not Cells A1 through A10. That's because there's a break in the values. Since Cell A6 is empty, Excel stopped at that point.

AutoSum is incredibly useful, but you do need to check the cell range it uses because of this, especially for really long data sets where you may not see the empty cell in your visible workspace.

(A quick note here that the AutoSum dropdown lets you do the same thing for AVERAGE, COUNT, MAX, and MIN. Also, AutoSum can be found on the left-hand side of the Formulas tab as well.)

Okay.

Let's move on to PRODUCT which is another simple one, although I would expect much less popular.

The PRODUCT Function

Notation:
PRODUCT(number1, [number2],…)

Excel Definition:
Multiplies all the numbers given as arguments.

The PRODUCT function does for multiplication what the SUM function does for addition. It will multiply all of the values that you include in the parens by one another.

A few examples:

=PRODUCT(2,3,4)

multiplies 2 times 3 times 4.

=PRODUCT(A1:A3)

multiplies the value in Cell A1 times the value in Cell A2 times the value in Cell A3.

=PRODUCT(A:A)

multiplies all of the values in Column A times one another. So Cell A1 times Cell A2 times Cell A3, etc.

The value of PRODUCT comes in when you have a large range of values that you need to multiply times one another. Of course, there aren't many circumstances where you'll want to multiply that many numbers times one another, which is why I suspect the function is rarely used.

The reason I've included it here is because of the next function we're going to discuss, SUMPRODUCT, which combines multiplying values and then summing the results into one function.

The SUMPRODUCT Function

Notation:
SUMPRODUCT(array1, [array2], [array3],...)

Excel Definition:
Returns the sum of the products of corresponding ranges or arrays.

Use SUMPRODUCT when you have a range of cells that need to be multiplied times one another and then where you want to take the sum of those results. So, for example, you want to multiply number of units times price to get a total cost per product, and then you want to sum those individual results to calculate a total cost.

You could get the same result using a combination of SUM and PRODUCT, which I'll show you in a minute, but why do so when SUMPRODUCT can shortcut the steps required.

You'll note in the notation for SUMPRODUCT it asks for arrays. An array is simply a range of cells. The key with a function like this that works with arrays is that they be the same size if there's more than one.

What SUMPRODUCT will do is take the first value from the first array and multiply that by the first value in the second array and store that result. It then does the same for the second value and the third and the fourth and on and on. At the end it takes all of those stored values and adds them together.

But for it to work there has to be n number of values in each array. If there aren't, you'll get a #VALUE! error.

Also, be sure that the ranges you choose have numbers in them and not text. Excel will treat non-numeric values as zeros and any number times zero is...zero.

Okay. Let's walk through an example. In Cells A1 through C4 we have our data. There are three products, each with a different amount of units sold, and a different price.

	A	B	C	D	E	F
1	Product	Quantity	Price	Total		Formula in Column D
2	Watchamacallits	10	$ 2.21	$ 22.10		=PRODUCT(B2:C2)
3	Whatsits	15	$ 2.40	$ 36.00		=PRODUCT(B3:C3)
4	Widgets	4	$ 3.00	$ 12.00		=PRODUCT(B4:C4)
5						
6			GRAND TOTAL	$ 70.10		=SUM(D2:D4)
7						
8			SUMPRODUCT	$ 70.10		=SUMPRODUCT(B2:B4,C2:C4)

I've placed the calculations in Column D and the corresponding formulas for those calculations in Column F so you can see the results and formulas at the same time.

Cells D2 through D6 show how you could use the PRODUCT and SUM functions separately to get the grand total for the three products. In Cells D2 through D4, the formula takes each individual row quantity and multiplies that times that row's price. The formula in Cell D6 then sums those values.

(Honestly, if I didn't want to also demonstrate a use of the PRODUCT function to you I would've just used the asterisk to multiply the values in Columns B and C.)

Cell D8 shows how the SUMPRODUCT function gets you the same exact result with one calculation:

$$=SUMPRODUCT(B2:B4,C2:C4)$$

The arrays that are used for the formula are the quantity and the price. So Excel takes the quantity for Watchamacallits and multiplies that by the price for Watchamacallits and stores the result. It then does the same for Whatsits and Widgets and when it's done that for all cells in those arrays it was provided it sums the stored results.

Simple enough and very useful if you need it.

Also, while the example I used above had two columns so two provided arrays, you are not limited to two arrays. If I also had sales tax as a column, I could've included that column as a third array in the formula.

You can also use SUMPRODUCT with values that are in rows instead of in columns.

You could even have arrays that cover more than one row and column, so a 2x2 range of cells, but then each array would have to be those same dimensions for it to work. (I can't honestly think of a situation where you'd want to do that. Maybe matrix math?)

But that does highlight the fact that your arrays need to match on both dimensions. If you have a column with three values and a row with three values, those won't work together without adjustment, because one is 1x3 and the other is 3x1.

In that instance, you could include the TRANSPOSE function in your SUMPRODUCT function to flip one or the other so they match up. For example:

$$=\text{SUMPRODUCT(B2:B4,TRANSPOSE(E11:G11))}$$

We'll talk about this more with the TRANSPOSE function, but what that does is takes the values in Cells E11 through G11, which stretch across three cells in a row and treats them as if they stretch across three cells in a column instead.

But that's a pretty obscure use of SUMPRODUCT, so let's move on to another very useful set of functions, AVERAGE and AVERAGEA.

The AVERAGE and AVERAGEA Functions

Notation:
AVERAGE(number1, [number2],…)

AVERAGEA(value1, [value2],…)

Excel Definition:
AVERAGE: Returns the average (arithmetic mean) of its arguments, which can be numbers or names, arrays, or references that contain numbers.

AVERAGEA: Returns the average (arithmetic mean) of its arguments, evaluating text and FALSE in arguments as 0; TRUE evaluates as 1. Arguments can be numbers, names, arrays, or references.

AVERAGE is one of the core calculations that Excel makes readily available. If you select a range of values in a worksheet, by default you should be able to see in the bottom right corner the average, count, and sum of the values in those cells.

And as we discussed above with AutoSum, the dropdown allows you to also create a formula for average.

So the Excel folks think it's one of the basic functions that a lot of people will want to use, which makes it important to understand.

I'm combining it here with AVERAGEA because there will be circumstances where AVERAGEA is the better choice and it's easier to show them together so you can see their differences.

First, let's clarify these somewhat confusing definitions.

Both the AVERAGE and AVERAGEA functions return the average (arithmetic mean) of their arguments.

The arguments can be numbers like 1, 2, 3, or 4. Or they can be a cell range, array of values, or even a named reference.

For AVERAGE, the values used in the function need to be numbers. AVERAGEA will also look at text or TRUE/FALSE values.

The AVERAGE function takes the sum of any numbers in the specified range and then divides that sum by the number of cells in the range that had a numeric value.

For example, if I have the values 1, 2, 3, 4, and 5 in a range of 5 cells from A1 through A5 and I write

$$=AVERAGE(A1:A5)$$

Excel will add those values to get 15, divide that total by 5, and return a value of 3.

If I include the blank cell Cell A6 in that range and write

$$=AVERAGE(A1:A6)$$

I will get the same result.

Even though I now have six cells in my range, because Cell A6 is blank, Excel ignores it. This is very important. And may not be what you wanted. (And happens also with AVERAGEA.)

If you have a cell in your range that should be included, you need to put a zero in that cell or it will not be included in your calculation.

If you use AVERAGE on a range of cells that include text in some of the cells, those cells that contain text will also be ignored and treated the same as a blank cell, so not counted for the divisor.

But if you use AVERAGEA those cells will be factored in. Each text entry will be treated as a zero value unless that text is TRUE, which is given a value of 1.

The table below provides different scenarios so you can see the two functions in action on the same data:

	A	B	C	D	E	F
1		AVERAGE and AVERAGEA Examples				
2		Scenario 1	Scenario 2	Scenario 3	Scenario 4	Scenario 5
3		1	1	1	1	TRUE
4		2	2	2	two	FALSE
5		3	3	3	3	FALSE
6		4	4	4	4	TRUE
7		5	5	5	5	TRUE
8				0		TRUE
9	AVERAGE Result	3.00	3.00	2.50	3.25	#DIV/0!
10	AVERAGE Formula	=AVERAGE(B3:B7)	=AVERAGE(C3:C8)	=AVERAGE(D3:D8)	=AVERAGE(E3:E8)	=AVERAGE(F3:F8)
11	# Cells In Range	5	6	6	6	6
12	Sum	15	15	15	13	0
13	Divide By	5	5	6	4	0
14						
15	AVERAGEA Result	3.00	3.00	2.50	2.60	0.67
16	AVERAGEA Formula	=AVERAGEA(B3:B7)	=AVERAGEA(C3:C8)	=AVERAGEA(D3:D8)	=AVERAGEA(E3:E8)	=AVERAGEA(F3:F8)
17	# Cells In Range	5	6	6	6	6
18	Sum	15	15	15	13	4
19	Divide By	5	5	6	5	6

Columns B through F contain various values in Rows 3 through 8.

In Rows 9 through 13 are the results and analysis for AVERAGE. In Rows 15 through 19 are the results and analysis for AVERAGEA.

The first row of each of those sections is the result of the formula used. So in Column B, both AVERAGE and AVERAGEA return the same result, 3. The next row shows the formula that was used. In the case of Column B, both formulas only referenced Rows 3 through 7.

Below that are three analysis rows. The first row, # Cells in Range, states how many cells were referenced in the formula. So the difference between Column B and Column C is that Column B's formulas only reference five cells, but Column C's expanded to include that blank cell in Row 8 so referenced six cells.

The next row, Sum, shows what that function considered the sum of the values. So in Column F, for example, you can see that AVERAGE considered those values to not be numbers to sum so the value was zero. But AVERAGEA considered the TRUE values to be equal to 1, so summed those entries to 4.

The final row, Divide By, shows how many cells the function used in its calculation. In Column C you can see that even though the number of cells in the range was six, both functions only counted five of those cells when making their calculation. But by adding a zero into Cell D8, the formulas in that column used six as the divisor.

It's a lot, I know. If you really need to know this spend some time with it. Otherwise, the big takeaway here is that the AVERAGE function may not work the way you think it does. Be sure for AVERAGE that there is a numeric value or a value of zero in each cell in the range that you want counted in the calculation.

And if you have any text values in your cell range or are using TRUE/FALSE results, you need to use AVERAGEA instead. Note that AVERAGEA also needs there to be something in each of those cells you want to count to work properly. It too will ignore blank cells.

Your best bet is to take a representative subset of your data where you can see what's happening and test the function you want to use on that subset to make sure that the result it gives you is what you expect.

You may need to use AVERAGEA instead of AVERAGE or you may need to take that data and apply a function to it to make it work properly. (Like an IFS or IF function to add a zero value to blank cells.) It will depend on your data.

Okay, next let's talk about a couple of alternatives to using an average: medians and modes.

The MEDIAN, MODE.SNGL, and MODE.MULT Functions

Notation:
MEDIAN(number1, [number2],…)

MODE.SNGL(number1, [number2],…)

MODE.MULT(number1, [number2],…)

Excel Definition:
MEDIAN: Returns the median, or the number in the middle of the set of given numbers.

MODE.SNGL: Returns the most frequently occurring, or repetitive, value in an array or range of data

MODE.MULT: Returns a vertical array of the most frequently occurring, or repetitive, values in an array or range of data.

AVERAGE is very useful and very commonly used. We often talk about the average of a range of values. Average income, average lifespan, etc. But an average can sometimes be very misleading. That's where MEDIAN and MODE come in. They often provide a more "true" result when there is some sort of skew in the data.

What do I mean by skew? Well, take writing for example. Or maybe acting is a more commonly-understood one. For every A-List star making millions there are hundreds if not thousands of actors who have to wait tables while they go on auditions and make next to nothing from their acting.

If you took the average income across ten actors, including one making a million, what you would see is a number that looks pretty good. "I can live on that."

But the problem is, those million-dollar actors are pulling the average up in an unrealistic way. Let's look at an example.

	A	B	C	D	E	F
1		**Income**				
2	Actor 1	$50.00				
3	Actor 2	$250.00		Average	$133,730.00	=AVERAGE(B2:B11)
4	Actor 3	$1,000.00		Median	$ 17,500.00	=MEDIAN(B2:B11)
5	Actor 4	$1,000.00		Mode (Single)	$ 1,000.00	=MODE.SNGL(B2:B11)
6	Actor 5	$10,000.00		Mode (Multiple)	$ 1,000.00	=MODE.MULT(B2:B11)
7	Actor 6	$25,000.00			$ 25,000.00	
8	Actor 7	$25,000.00				
9	Actor 8	$100,000.00				
10	Actor 9	$175,000.00				
11	Actor 10	$1,000,000.00				

In Cells B2 through B11 in the above screenshot are incomes for various actors. They range from $50 to $1,000,000. The average across all ten values, shown in Cell E3 is $133,730. I could live on that.

But.

All except for two of the actors in that table are earning less than that. That's what it means to have a value skew the result. That million-dollar actor makes it look livable to be an actor.

So how else could you look at these numbers and come up with some sort of generalization?

One way is to split the results in the middle. What does the middle person earn? That's what the MEDIAN function is meant to give you.

If there is a middle value, so if I had nine entries instead of ten, that would be the fifth value. Excel would return that middle value.

If there are an even number of observations, like we see here, then it takes the values on either side and averages them. The MEDIAN you see here is the average of $10,000 and $25,000, the incomes for Actors 5 and 6.

Which means median has its weakness, too. Because say you had two possible outcomes, $1,000 and $100,000. The median result would be $50,500 but that isn't at all possible. You either make it, $100,000, or you don't, $1,000. If you were betting on overall outcomes, knowing the median would help, but if you personally needed to know whether to take that risk, you'd need to understand that your outcomes are actually either $1,000 or $100,000.

The mode functions, MODE.SNGL and MODE.MULT can sometimes help with a scenario like that.

What MODE.SNGL does is tells you the single-most frequently occurring value in the range. MODE.MULT tells you all values that occur at that frequency.

Both are specific to a value. So they treat $1,000 and $1,010 and $1,050 as different values. Which may generate a misleading result if your data is something like income that can have minor differences between values.

The mode functions are best with data where there are discrete outcomes. For example, *there are five possible results, which is the most common?* They do require numbers, but you could assign a number to each outcome. What is the most common profession, baker (1), mechanic (2), or doctor (3)? A result of 2, would mean mechanic is the most common.

If two values occur with equal frequency, MODE.SNGL only returns the first one it finds. You can see this in Cell E5.

The problem is, in the table above both $1,000 and $25,000 occur twice. They are both the most frequent result. Better to use MODE.MULT and see both results.

MODE.MULT is what's called an array function, meaning it can return more than one value. What's nice is that in current versions of Excel you enter that function just like you would any other and then hit enter and it does its thing.

(Before that change you had to select the cells where the results would go in advance and be sure to hit Enter in a special way. It was a pain.)

It's important to know which functions are array functions, because you need to leave room for them to provide their results.

Here, for example, is what happened when I used MODE.MULT and it had two results for me:

Excel displayed a message that the formula had returned multiple values and as result they were spilled to neighboring blank cells. I was fine with that, so I clicked on "Got It".

If I'd had text below that first cell, Excel would've generated an error, like this one:

I put text in the cell directly below my MODE.MULT formula and so it had nowhere to put the second result when I hit enter so generated a #SPILL! error message.

When I clicked back onto Cell E6, Excel showed a dotted line around the cell that contained the content that was in the way, letting me know what needed moved or deleted.

As soon as I clicked into Cell E7 and deleted that text Excel displayed the results of the formula.

The way that Excel now shows an array formula has also changed. The main cell where the original formula was entered, in this case Cell E6, looks like any other cell with a formula in it.

But Cell E7 which contains the "spilled" results of the formula has the formula grayed out in the formula bar:

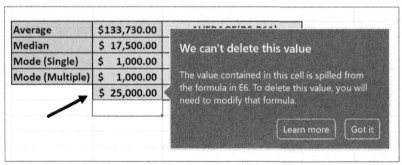

I can see what formula is populating the value in Cell E7, but I can't edit it. And if I type into Cell E7 it treats that as text that was entered into the cell and deletes the formula and erases the result. It also brings back the spill error in Cell E6.

If you try to delete the value, it will give an error message:

Note that the error message is nice enough to tell you which cell to go to, Cell E6, to make any edits to the formula. Pretty cool, huh?

Okay, so let's sum this up.

AVERAGE takes the total of the range of values and divides by the number of values.

MEDIAN returns the middle value in a range. If no middle exists because there's an even number of values, it will average the middle two values and return that average.

MODE.SNGL returns one value that is the most frequently occurring value.

(Note that MODE.SNGL replaced the MODE function so MODE works the exact same way but Excel has flagged it as a function that is only kept to be compatible with older versions of Excel.)

MODE.MULT returns the most frequently occurring values, however many there are.

Each has its strengths, each has its weaknesses. The best way to understand which one to use is often to plot your data. Also, with the mode functions, you may want to bucket your results if there are a lot of similar but not identical values. So in our example above, I could use an IFS function to assign each income level to a "bin" of 1, 2, 3, or 4 and then use MODE on those bins to see which is most common.

But we can also use a function called FREQUENCY to do something similar, so let's looks at that next.

The FREQUENCY Function

Notation:
FREQUENCY(data_array,bins_array)

Excel Definition:
Calculates how often values occur within a range of values and then returns a vertical array of numbers having one more element than Bins_array.

That definition sounds like a lot of gibberish, right? Let's see if we can't rephrase it.

Basically, what that definition means is that the FREQUENCY function will look at a range you provide (the data_array) and then it will tell you how many of the values fall within the ranges you specify. The way you specify those ranges is by creating a bins_array which is essentially a range of cells that have values that set the boundary of your bins.

Let's look at a couple of examples.

Here we have the same data from the last chapter where we looked at medians and modes.

	A	B	C	D	E	F	G
1		Income			Bins	Frequency	
2	Actor 1	$50.00			$10,000	5	=FREQUENCY(B2:B11,E2:E4)
3	Actor 2	$250.00			$25,000	2	
4	Actor 3	$1,000.00			$100,000	1	
5	Actor 4	$1,000.00			>$100,000	2	
6	Actor 5	$10,000.00					
7	Actor 6	$25,000.00			Bins	Frequency	
8	Actor 7	$25,000.00			$50.00	1	=FREQUENCY(B2:B11,E8:E15)
9	Actor 8	$100,000.00			$250.00	1	
10	Actor 9	$175,000.00			$1,000.00	2	
11	Actor 10	$1,000,000.00			$10,000.00	1	
12					$25,000.00	2	
13					$100,000.00	1	
14					$175,000.00	1	
15					$1,000,000.00	1	
16						0	

What I have done in Column E is created two different sets of "bins" for the FREQUENCY function to use. The first set of bins is in Cells E2 through E4.

Note that I said E4 not E5.

Each of the values I put into those cells was arbitrary. I thought $10,000, $25,000, and $100,000 were good cutoff marks. I could have used any value I wanted.

What I put in Cell E5 was just text for me, it's not used by the function.

Here's the FREQUENCY function for that first set of bins:

=FREQUENCY(B2:B11,E2:E4)

What that is saying is, "Look at the values in Cells B2 through B11 and for each numeric value you find place it in one of the bins specified in Cells E2 through E4 where the first bin is defined as the value in Cell E2 or any value less than that, the next bin is any value greater than the value in Cell E2 up to the value in Cell E3, the next bin is greater than the value in Cell E3 and up to the value in Cell E4, and the next value is anything over the value in Cell E4."

The FREQUENCY function provides one more result than the number of bins you set, because the final count is essentially "any values greater than the value in the last cell listed in the bins array."

In that first table, I went ahead and labeled it just to remind myself of what that count covers. But what I put in Cell E5 is not part of the formula.

Now let's look at the second table there. What I did with that one is I took my values in Column B and copied them to Column E and then I removed duplicate values. I then used this formula in Cell F8:

=FREQUENCY(B2:B11,E8:E15)

Once more that is going to look at the values in Column B, but now it is going to count those values based upon the values in Cells E8 through E15, which are the unique values in my data. Which means what I'm getting in Cells F8 through F16 are the counts for each of the unique values in my data. It is still technically a range, but because of the way I chose my bins all of the data points are exactly equal to the values listed in that table.

And because that's how it works, it adds that last value in Cell F16 for anything greater than $1,000,000 but there are none, so that final result is 0.

FREQUENCY is also an array function, so you have to leave it room to work. Basically, if you put the function where I did, which is in the same row as your first bins array value, you need one cell below the last bins array value for the function to provide your results. If you block that last spot, you will get a SPILL error and no result.

Also, keep in mind that in prior versions of Excel array functions worked very differently than they do now. They were much more cumbersome to deal with. Now you just type an array function in like a normal function and hit enter and it works as long as you gave it enough space to work in.

Finally, FREQUENCY ignores blank cells and text, so it can only be used with numeric values.

The nice thing about FREQUENCY is that you can then use that data table to create a quick column chart to visually represent the distribution of the results. Here I've used that first table of results to create a quick column chart, for example:

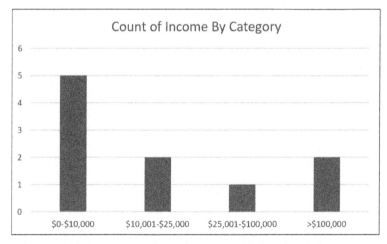

(Although I do recommend copying and pasting special after you have your results, so you can then change the labels on your bins like I have here.)

This graph makes it pretty clear that the most likely outcome for our actors is an income under $10,000. I'd say it's much more clear than the use of AVERAGE, MEDIAN, or one of the mode functions made it. Of course, I made up the data and I chose the bins to use, so there's that.

Okay, on to MIN.

The MIN and MINA Functions

Notation:
MIN(number1, [number2],…)

MINA(value1, [value2],…)

Excel Definition:
MIN: Returns the smallest number in a set of values. Ignores logical values and text.

MINA: Returns the smallest value in a set of values. Does not ignore logical values and text.

The MIN and MINA functions take a range of values and return the smallest value in the range. The difference between the two is that MIN only works on numbers whereas MINA will also work on text or TRUE/FALSE results.

MINA assigns a value of 0 to text and FALSE and a value of 1 to TRUE.

If there are no numbers in a range for MIN it will return a result of zero.

Likewise, if there are no *values* in a range for MINA it will return a result of zero.

If there is an error in the range, the function will return that error as well. So, for example, I tried applying it to the FREQUENCY function from the last section and then created a spill error in that FREQUENCY function and my result displayed as #SPILL!

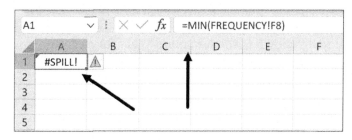

I show this to you for another reason, because I also want to show you how to apply a function like this one to a range of values generated by an array function. Look at the formula I used:

=MIN(FREQUENCY!F8)

The portion in parens, FREQUENCY!F8, is referencing Cell F8 in the worksheet titled FREQUENCY. That cell contains an array function that returned nine values, but you don't reference the cells that contain those values. You only reference the one that contains the array formula.

On a more normal data set, you would reference the cell range that contains your values. For example, to take the minimum of the values in Column A I would write:

=MIN(A:A)

Here are some more examples:

	A	B	C	D	E	F
1			MIN		MINA	
2		Scenario 1	Scenario 2	Scenario 3	Scenario 4	Scenario 5
3		#DIV/0!	4	-2	TRUE	test
4		1	1	1	2	1
5		2	2	2	3	2
6		3	3	3	4	3
7		4	5	4	5	5
8		5	6	5	6	6
9	Result	#DIV/0!	1.00	-2.00	1.00	0.00
10	Formula	=MIN(B3:B8)	=MIN(C3:C8)	=MIN(D3:D8)	=MINA(E3:E8)	=MINA(F3:F8)

Pay attention to what I have in the first row of each of the examples.

In Column B there is an error message in Cell B1 therefore the result of using MIN on that range is the error message.

In Column C it's just a regular number, so Excel looks at the range of values and returns a minimum value of 1.

In Column D there's a negative number so it's the minimum value.

Column E uses the MINA function instead and the first value in the range is TRUE, which gets a value of 1 and that's shown as the minimum value for that range.

Column F also uses the MINA function but the first value is random text, in this case, "test", which is assigned a value of 0 which is the minimum value in the range of cells.

Once again, if you're not sure which one to use, take a small enough range of your data that you can see what's happening, like I did above, and then apply MIN or MINA to the range to see what happens and if that's what you thought would happen.

Okay. On to MAX.

The MAX and MAXA Functions

Notation:
MAX(number1, [number2],…)

MAXA(value1, [value2],…)

Excel Definition:
MAX: Returns the largest value in a set of values. Ignores logical values and text.

MAXA: Returns the largest value in a set of values. Does not ignore logical values and text.

MAX and MAXA work exactly like MIN and MINA except they return the maximum, or largest value. If there are no numbers (MAX) or values (MAXA) in the range, the result is zero. MAX ignores text entries and does not include logical values such as TRUE/FALSE. MAXA treats text entries and FALSE as equivalent to 0 and TRUE as equivalent to 1.

If there is an error message in the range, both functions will return the error message.

Here are some examples:

	A	B	C	D	E	F
1		MAX			MAXA	
2		Scenario 1	Scenario 2	Scenario 3	Scenario 4	Scenario 5
3		-2	#DIV/0!	-2	-2	-2
4		1	1	-1	-1	-1
5		2	2	0	0	-3
6		3	3	TRUE	TRUE	test
7		4	5	FALSE	FALSE	
8		5	6			
9	Result	5.00	#DIV/0!	0.00	1.00	0.00
10	Formula	=MAX(B3:B8)	=MAX(C3:C8)	=MAX(D3:D8)	=MAXA(E3:E8)	=MAXA(F3:F8)

Column B is a simple example using MAX and values that range from -2 to 5. The maximum value returned is 5.

Column C has an error message in one of the cell ranges so returns that same error message as its result.

Column D is using MAX so the TRUE and FALSE results are ignored which leaves a maximum value of 0.

Column E is that same data using MAXA so the maximum value is 1 because TRUE is assigned a value of 1.

Column F includes random text which is assigned a value of 0 and so is considered the maximum value for the range.

When in doubt about which to use, test it out. Okay, on to ROUND.

The ROUND, ROUNDUP, and ROUNDDOWN Functions

Notation:
ROUND(number, num_digits)

ROUNDUP(number, num_digits)

ROUNDDOWN(number, num_digits)

Excel Definition:
ROUND: Rounds a number to a specified number of digits.

ROUNDUP: Rounds a number up, away from zero.

ROUNDDOWN: Rounds a number down, towards zero.

I used the ROUND function in the introductory chapters, because this is one I use often. With my publishing I receive reports from vendors that are in various currencies. Each month with Amazon alone I can have sales in USD, GBP, AUD, CAD, MXN, JPY, EUR, and more.

I always convert those values to my currency, USD, because especially with currencies like Japanese Yen (JPY) that makes a very big difference. As I write this, 1 JPY is equivalent to .0073 USD. Which means when I look in my reports and see 450 JPY it seems really exciting until I convert that and find out it's basically three dollars U.S.

The problem with the formula I use to convert, which is just the JPY amount times the conversion rate, is that I end up with lots of decimal places sometimes. For example, 450 times .0073 is 3.285. But I want that amount in currency. Amazon isn't paying me half a cent.

If I format it to look like currency, that doesn't help, because it still retains that information in the background. But ROUND will convert it into a number with just two decimal places.

I sometimes run into the same issue with how they report KU page reads and what I've earned on those, because they are actually paying half a cent or less per page read and will report it as such. So they'll tell me I earned 1.23456 on some book, but we both know that's not what they're going to pay me.

Taking those values and wrapping ROUND around them solves my problem, because it lets me convert them to a value with only two decimal places.

Here's an example using ROUND and that Japanese Yen conversion rate, assuming that the value earned in JPY is in Cell A1:

$$=ROUND(A1*.0073,2)$$

Note here that the first input is actually a calculation. I'm having Excel convert from JPY to USD inside the formula.

You can absolutely do that with any formula and function. Just be careful that you keep the calculation isolated to the portion of the function that's reserved for that input.

You can see I did that here because the calculation was kept between the opening paren and the first comma. In some instances, you may need to use parens around the calculation to do that, especially if the calculation includes a comma.

The second input is the number of digits to display from the decimal, which is 2 in this example.

You can actually use a negative value for number of digits to get just the 100s or just the 1000s out of a number. If you ever look at financial reporting for really large companies, they do this. They do not put that they earned $11,232,121,121.23 in a report. They put that they earned $11,232 millions.

We'll look at that more in a moment when we walk through the examples in the table below.

Note here that I used the ROUND function. Under normal circumstances, that's the one to use because it balances out any potential rounding errors. ROUND takes values that are 5 or more and rounds those up. It takes values under 5 and rounds them down. Over a large number of observations, this evens out.

The ROUNDUP and ROUNDDOWN functions force the direction that Excel rounds in. They will always round in one direction and one direction only, which means that they will introduce bias into your grand total over a large number of observations.

There are times to use them, however. For example, when budgeting I like to always round my income down and round my expenses up so that I always have slightly more money than I thought I would. (That little trick saved me more than once in college.)

Okay. Let's look at a table of values now to see how these functions work and how they differ in terms of how they handle rounding:

	A	B	C	D	E
1	Value	Decimal Places	ROUND	ROUNDUP	ROUNDDOWN
2	3.124	2	3.12	3.13	3.12
3	3.126	2	3.13	3.13	3.12
4	-3.1246	2	-3.12	-3.13	-3.12
5	-3.1262	2	-3.13	-3.13	-3.12
6	12126.25	-2	12100	12200	12100
7	12167.36	-2	12200	12200	12100
8	-251234.81	-4	-250000	-260000	-250000
9	-256234.81	-4	-260000	-260000	-250000
10		Row 2 Formula	=ROUND(A2,B2)	=ROUNDUP(A2,B2)	=ROUNDDOWN(A2,B2)

In Column A I've listed various values. Column B says how many decimal places we're going to round to. Column C does that using the ROUND function, Column D does that using the ROUNDUP function. Column E does that using the ROUNDDOWN function.

In Row 10 you can see the text of the formulas used in Row 2. Adjust the cell references for each line and you'll have the formula used for each of the other rows. (I just copied and let Excel do that for me.)

Notice that there is not a single value where they all three come up with the same result. I think the only time they would is if there was no rounding required. So if that first value were 3.12 with no further decimal places, then all three would return the value 3.12. But otherwise ROUNDUP and ROUNDDOWN will always move opposite each other.

When you tell Excel to round a value using a positive number for the number of digits, it keeps the number as-is up to that point and then uses the number one past that to decide whether to round up or down.

So, for those first two entries, 3.124 and 3.126, Excel starts with the value 3.12.

For ROUND it then looks at the next digit, the 4 or the 6, and it decides whether the 3.12 stands (rounding down) or whether it needs to increase by one (rounding up) to 3.13.

Under 5, the number stays. 5 or more, the number goes up. That's why the value in Cell C2 is 3.12, because the next digit is a 4. And why the value in Cell C3 is 3.13, because the next digit is a 6.

For ROUNDUP and ROUNDDOWN that next digit, as long as it isn't zero, is irrelevant. If there's any digit other than zero, then Excel goes up or goes down depending on which function was used. You can see that in Cells D2 and D3 and E2 and E3 where the ROUNDUP and ROUNDDOWN functions returned the same result for both values.

ROUNDUP rounded up to 3.13. ROUNDDOWN rounded down to 3.12.

As I mentioned above, the number of digits can also be a negative number.

That works a little differently. In that case, Excel counts to the left from the decimal the number of digits specified and then keeps everything to the left of that point and uses the digit it counted to to determine how to round.

We can see this in Rows 6 and 7.

Rows 6 and 7 use -2 for the digits and the values 12126.25 and 12167.36, respectively. Counting 2 digits to the left of the decimal place and then keeping everything to the left leaves us with 12100 to start. Excel is either going to leave that 12100 or round up to 12200 based on the tens value in each number and the function used.

As long as that number isn't a zero, ROUNDDOWN gives 12100 and ROUNDUP gives 12200.

ROUND takes the 2 in the tens spot from 12126.25 and rounds down to 12100 but takes the 6 in the tens spot in 12167.36 and rounds up to 12200.

The other thing I want to point out in this chart is how negative numbers work. We have those values in Rows 4 and 5 and in Rows 8 and 9.

For all four rows, ROUNDUP and ROUNDDOWN basically return the same result you would expect if the number were positive and then just add a negative in front of the result.

To me that's a bit counterintuitive because of their names. When I think of "up" I think, "return the larger value". For a negative value that would mean, round *towards* zero. Because -3.12 is a larger number than -3.13.

But as you can see, that's not what happens.

Look again at how Excel describes the functions. ROUNDUP rounds "away from zero" and ROUNDDOWN rounds "towards zero." They should maybe more appropriately be called ROUNDAWAY and ROUNDTO.

Hopefully you are never in a situation where that little bit of nuance becomes important, but I wanted to point it out, just in case.

Now on to another core function in Excel, COUNT.

The COUNT, COUNTA, and COUNTBLANK Functions

Notation:

COUNT(value1, [value2],…)

COUNTA(value1, [value2],…)

COUNTBLANK(range)

Excel Definition:

COUNT: Counts the number of cells in a range that contain numbers.

COUNTA: Counts the number of cells in a range that are not empty.

COUNTBLANK: Counts the number of empty cells in a specified range of cells.

COUNT is another one of those popular default functions in Excel. The result of the COUNT function appears in the bottom of your workspace when you select a range of cells, alongside AVERAGE and SUM, and it's one of the functions that pivot tables default to using, too.

Which means it's important to understand how it works. What COUNT does is it allows you to count how many cells within your specified range contain a number or a date.

So a range of cells that contain the values 1, 12/31/10, and "one" will be counted as 2 because the first two entries (1 and 12/13/10) are considered numbers, but the last entry ("one") is not.

If you have a cell that shows a numeric value due to a formula, so the cell contents are actually =SUM(2,3) but the cell displays 5, that will be counted as well.

Excel says that it will also count an entry such as "1" as a number, but when I tried that it didn't work. So if you're going to use this function on a range, I would test it on a subset of your data to make sure that it's counting your entries properly.

Also, to be counted a cell can *only* contain a number or date. For example, "1 day" would not be counted since it includes the number 1 but also the text "day".

The COUNT function itself is very simple to use. For example,

$$=COUNT(A1:A5)$$

will count the number of cells in the range from Cell A1 through Cell A5 that contain a number or date.

You could also write a function such as

$$=COUNT(1,2,3)$$

and it would count the number of numbers or dates in the list within the parens. In this case, three.

If you don't want to limit your count to just numbers and dates, then you need to use COUNTA which counts how many cells in the range are not empty.

So, for example, COUNTA will count the cell that has "1 day" in it as well as the cell that has a date or a number or the text "one". Anything in a cell will result in that cell being counted.

Be careful, however, because it will also count any cell that has a function in it even if that function is not currently displaying a value. (And using copy and then paste special – values to replace that function may not clear the cell enough for COUNTA to ignore it. You have to make sure that a cell is truly blank for it to not be counted by using the Clear option.)

Once again, if you're going to use this, test it on a small range to make sure that it works as expected.

The reverse of COUNTA is theoretically COUNTBLANK.

According to Excel, formulas that return empty text ("") are counted as blank, but cells with zero values are not. I tested this with an IF function that returned a value of "", a value of " ", and a value of 0. The one that returned a value of "" was counted as blank, the other two were not.

This is important to know because a cell with a formula that returns a value of "" and one with a formula that returns a value of " " will look the same, but they perform differently when functions like this one are applied to them.

That also means that COUNTA and COUNTBLANK may end up counting the same cell because COUNTBLANK may see the result of a function as an empty cell at the same time COUNTA sees the formula.

As always, be sure to check a sample of your data to see that the result you are getting is the result you expect and want. If it isn't, you should look to the nature of your data.

Here is some sample data and how Excel counted it with each of the functions:

	A	B	C	D	E	F
1	**Values**					
2	1			**COUNT**	**3**	**=COUNT(A2:A10)**
3	1/2/2010			**COUNTA**	**8**	**=COUNTA(A2:A10)**
4	"1"			**COUNTBLANK**	**2**	**=COUNTBLANK(A2:A10)**
5	one					
6	1 day					
7		Formula returning " "				
8		Formula returning ""				
9	0	Formula =C9				
10		Blank Cell				

The COUNT function counted a date or number in Cells A2, A3, and A9. (I could tell which one it was counting by deleting the various values and seeing how the result changed. It does not count the "1" value which likely means that help text is referring to the result of importing a .csv file or something similar where it's actually different to Excel than my typing in "1" in a cell.)

The COUNTA function counted everything except for the truly blank cell. So those two formulas that are currently returning a "" and a " ", respectively, were both counted.

If COUNTBLANK were actually the COUNTA counterpart it would only show a count of 1. But it instead counts two cells, the truly blank one in Cell A10 as well as the one that contains a formula that returns a value of "".

So there you have it. The ins and outs of the basic count functions. Next let's talk about LARGE and SMALL, two that I don't use often but could be handy if ever needed.

The LARGE and SMALL Functions

Notation:

LARGE(array, k)

SMALL(array, k)

Excel Definition:

LARGE: Returns the k-th largest value in a data set. For example, the fifth largest number.

SMALL: Returns the k-th smallest value in a data set. For example, the fifth smallest number.

The LARGE and SMALL functions can actually be interchangeable if you know the size of your data.

What they do is look at a range of values and return the nth (or kth according to the definition) largest or smallest value in that range. And since the largest value in a 10-value range is also the 10th smallest value, you can basically use either one to get your result.

They're both very straightforward. The first input is the range where you want to find the largest or smallest value. The second input is a number representing the position within that range. 3 for the 3rd largest or smallest, 5 for the fifth largest or smallest, etc.

Here are a few examples:

	A	B		C	D	E	F
1	123				1	5	10
2	234			LARGE	12134	123	1
3	1			SMALL	1	23	12134
4	23						
5	5678			*Formula in Column D*			
6	12			LARGE	=LARGE($A$1:$A$10,D1)		
7	5			SMALL	=SMALL($A$1:$A$10,D1)		
8	6						
9	12134						
10	232						

You can see that I have an unsorted list of values in Column A that range from 1 to 12134. I created a small table in Cells C1 to F3 where I could then apply the LARGE and SMALL functions to that data using different values for k.

Because I know that there are 10 values in that list in Column A I also know that the 10th smallest value should match my largest value and vice versa. Which you can see in that table. But because I have an even number of values in my data range, the 5th largest value is not the same as the 5th smallest value. Those values are positions 5 and 6 in the range and depending on which direction you're coming from you'll get either 123 as the 5th largest value or 23 as the 5th smallest value.

You can see the formulas I used for Column D in Rows 6 and 7. Because I wrote those formulas using $ signs to fix the Column A cell range reference, I was able to just copy and paste each formula to Columns E and F and let Excel adjust the rest of the formula for me.

Okay. Now on to RANK. (Or the new versions, RANK.AVG and RANK.EQ.)

The RANK.AVG and RANK.EQ Functions

Notation:
RANK.EQ(number, ref, [order])

RANK.AVG(number, ref, [order])

Excel Definition:
RANK.EQ: Returns the rank of a number in a list of numbers: its size relative to other values in the list; if more than one value has the same rank, the top rank of that set of values is returned.

RANK.AVG: Returns the rank of a number in a list of numbers: its size relative to other values in the list; if more than one value has the same rank, the average rank is returned.

RANK.EQ is the same as the original Excel function RANK which has since been retired. It differs from RANK.AVG in terms of how the two functions handle situations where multiple values share the same rank, which we'll talk about at the end.

Where SMALL and LARGE look at a range of data and return the nth value in that range, RANK.EQ and RANK.AVG look at a range of data and tell you where a specific value ranks within that range.

So here's the same data we used for SMALL and LARGE but this time I've swapped out what the table is looking for. I've used the values that SMALL and LARGE found for us instead. That means the results you're seeing in that table are the rank for each of those values in our data range.

	A	B	C	D	E	F	G
1	123			12134	123	1	23
2	234		RANK.EQ	1	5	10	6
3	1		RANK.AVG	1	5	10	6
4	23						
5	5678			Formula in Column D			
6	12		RANK.EQ	=RANK.EQ(D$1,$A$1:$A$10)			
7	5		RANK.AVG	=RANK.AVG(D$1,$A$1:$A$10)			
8	6						
9	12134						
10	232						

By default, the value 12134 ranks as 1 and the value 1 ranks as 10. I left out the last input to the functions, order, which is an optional input. When you do that, the default in Excel is to sort the data from largest to smallest so that the largest value (12134) is the top-ranked value and the smallest value (1) is the lowest-ranked value.

You can change that by using a 1 for the last input into the function. So if I change the RANK.EQ formula for Cell D2 to:

=RANK.EQ(D$1,$A$1:$A$10,1)

that will change the result to 10 for the value of 12134 because Excel will sort the data from smallest to largest putting 12134 at the end of the list, or the 10th spot.

Note that the data once again is not required to be sorted before the functions work so you can use them on any data range you want without having to prepare that data first.

Now let's talk about how they differ. That requires new data. Because we need duplicate values to see the difference between the two functions.

Here I have changed our data over to student test scores. The top result was a 99, the lowest was a 92. The formulas do not change, but because the data changed the results that RANK.EQ and RANK.AVG return are different.

	A	B	C	D	E	F	G
1	99			99	98	97	92
2	98		RANK.EQ	1.0	2.0	4.0	7.0
3	98		RANK.AVG	1.0	2.5	4.5	8.5
4	97						
5	97			Formula in Column D			
6	95		RANK.EQ	=RANK.EQ(D$1,$A$1:$A$10)			
7	92		RANK.AVG	=RANK.AVG(D$1,$A$1:$A$10)			
8	92						
9	92						
10	92						

Let's walk through these results so we can understand why.

The first one is fine. There's only one student who got a 99 and it's the top result, so both functions agree that student was the top score, the 1st rank.

The second one we get different results because two students scored 98, which means the second rank is someone who scored a 98, but so is the third rank. RANK.EQ gives both of the students a rank of 2, the highest possible rank given their score. RANK.AVG takes the average of the possible ranks and gives that to the score. Since 2 and 3 were the options, RANK.AVG returns 5/2 which is 2.5.

The same thing happens for 97 where two students scored 97 and that's the fourth and fifth position in the ranking. RANK.EQ gives the best-case scenario of 4, RANK.AVG gives the average of 4.5.

For the final value, 92, which we see in Column G, there are four students with that score. They are the 7th, 8th, 9th, and 10th ranks. RANK.EQ gives the best rank, 7. RANK.AVG adds 7, 8, 9, and 10 and then divides by 4 to get 8.5.

One final point, be sure to format your values so you can see the decimal places when using the RANK.AVG function or else you might miss what the true rank it's returning is.

Now let's learn how to generate random numbers.

The RAND and RANDBETWEEN Functions

Notation:
RAND()

RANDBETWEEN(bottom, top)

Excel Definition:
RAND: Returns a random number greater than or equal to 0 and less than 1, evenly distributed. (Changes on recalculation.)

RANDBETWEEN: Returns a random number between the numbers you specify.

RAND and RANDBETWEEN are both functions that generate random numbers. If I need some quick random data, I use one of these.

A key difference between them is that RAND returns decimal values between 0 and 1. So 0.523134, 0.467156, 0.992111, etc. From what I'm seeing right now it looks like it defaults to a number with fifteen decimal places, six of which are visible in the worksheet by default.

RANDBETWEEN, on the other hand, returns integers. So if I give it a bottom value of 0 and a top value of 1 the only two possible results are 0 and 1. It does not return decimal values.

The bottom value input to RANDBETWEEN is defined by Excel as "the smallest integer RANDBETWEEN will return". The top value input is defined as "the largest integer RANDBETWEEN will return". If the bottom value you provide is not smaller than the top value, Excel will generate a #NUM! error so be careful to get your range in the right order.

Both functions will continue to update with new random values if you leave them sitting there. Type text in a cell, hit enter, and boom they're showing a different result. Use F9, different result. Reopen your worksheet, different result. (Unless you have that setting turned off.)

And you cannot go back to the prior random result if that happens. Not even with Undo. Excel is not storing those random values anywhere so if you use Ctrl + Z it just generates a new random value.

To prevent a random number from changing, I will copy and paste special-values to lock in my set of random values and remove the function.

You can also click into the cell with the formula in it, highlight the portion that calculates your random value, RAND( ), for example, without the equals sign, and then use F9. That converts that portion of that formula into its result. It also removes the function.

I should note here, too, that RAND is the first function we've seen that doesn't require an input. If all you want is that random number in a cell, then you can just write RAND() with an equals sign before it. (I can't show you that here in Word or it generates random text on me.)

In the past, I would often pair RAND with something like ROUND and multiplication. So:

$$=ROUND(RAND()*100,0)$$

That formula generates a random whole number between 0 and 100. Note how no matter where RAND appears in the formula it needs those opening and closing parens to work.

Now I am much more likely to use RANDBETWEEN. I can get the same result with:

$$=RANDBETWEEN(0,100)$$

Note that if you have both of those formulas in the same worksheet, even though they're both doing the same thing—generating a random whole number between 0 and 100—they won't generate the same value.

Okay, let's move away from numbers for a bit and turn our attention to some simple functions that manipulate text.

The UPPER, LOWER, and PROPER Functions

Notation:

UPPER(text)

LOWER(text)

PROPER(text)

Excel Definition:

UPPER: Converts a text string to all uppercase letters.

LOWER: Converts all letters in a text string to lowercase.

PROPER: Converts a text string to proper case; the first letter in each word to uppercase, and all other letters to lowercase.

The UPPER, LOWER, and PROPER functions all work the same way. They take an inputted text string and apply formatting to that text. For UPPER, the text is placed into all caps. For LOWER it is changed to all lower case. And for PROPER it is changed so that the first letter in each word is uppercase and then all other letters are lowercase.

You can see examples for two sets of text, "Hello, how are you" and "this is a mess", for each function here:

◢	A	B	C	D
1	Sample Text	UPPER	LOWER	PROPER
2	Hello, how are you	HELLO, HOW ARE YOU	hello, how are you	Hello, How Are You
3	this is a mess	THIS IS A MESS	this is a mess	This Is A Mess
4				
5	Formula In Row 2	=UPPER(A2)	=LOWER(A2)	=PROPER(A2)
6				
7		HELLO, HOW ARE YOU THIS IS A MESS	hello, how are you this is a mess	Hello, How Are You This Is A Mess
8	Formula In Row 7	=UPPER(TEXTJOIN(" ",TRUE,A2,A3))	=LOWER(TEXTJOIN(" ",TRUE,A2,A3))	=PROPER(TEXTJOIN(" ",TRUE,A2,A3))

Column A contains the text, Column B contains the results for UPPER, Column C contains the results for LOWER, and Column D contains the results for PROPER.

Row 5 shows the formula used to produce the values in Row 2. Very simple.

Each function only takes one input. In the examples above I used a cell reference, but you could also input the text directly into the function by using quotation marks around the text. Like this:

=UPPER("Hello, how are you")

That will give you HELLO, HOW ARE YOU as well.

You can get around the fact that the functions each only work with one cell reference or one phrase by joining them with another function. We haven't covered it yet, but I did that in the image above using the TEXTJOIN function.

You can see the result of combining the text in Cells A2 and A3 and then applying each function in Row 7. And the formulas I used to do this in Row 8. Here is what I used for UPPER:

=UPPER(TEXTJOIN(" ",TRUE,A2,A3))

That looks complicated but it's basically UPPER placed around the other function. So you have the opening paren, and then the other function (in this case TEXTJOIN) and all of its inputs (in this case (" ",TRUE,A2,A3), and then the closing paren. And that lets you get around the one-input limit for each of these functions.

(CONCATENATE and CONCAT are other functions that you could use to join multiple sections of text at once if you don't have access to TEXTJOIN, which is a new function introduced in Excel 2019.)

Keep in mind when you use UPPER, LOWER, and PROPER that the result may look like text but is in fact a formula. Use paste special-values to lock in the results as text only.

The LEN Function

Notation:
LEN(text)

Excel Definition:
Returns the number of characters in a text string.

The LEN (or length as I think of it) function is one that provides information that can be used elsewhere. I'll show you how that works in a minute when we talk about LEFT, RIGHT, and MID.

What it does is returns for you a count of the number of characters in a text string. You can either provide the text directly into the function or you can have a cell that contains that text that you then reference. So:

=LEN("test")

will return a result of 4 as will

=LEN(A1)

if the word test is in Cell A1.

Both are legitimate formulas that use the LEN function. Note that if you use text directly in the function you have to put that text into quotes or else you will get a #NAME? error. And also that it then ignores the quote marks when counting the number of characters.

If there is a formula in the referenced cell, LEN looks at the result of that formula not the text in the formula. (Which makes sense, I'm just telling you how it works.)

And if a cell is empty or has a "" value, then LEN will return a value of zero.

LEN has a counterpart, LENB, that works for languages like Japanese, Chinese, or Korean. It counts the number of bytes in the text string as opposed to the number of characters.

Let's talk about LEFT, RIGHT, and MID now and then show how to combine those with LEN to extract parts of a text string.

The LEFT, RIGHT, and MID Functions

Notation:

LEFT(text, [num_chars])

RIGHT(text, [num_chars])

MID(text, start_num, num_chars)

Excel Definition:

LEFT: Returns the specified number of characters from the start of a text string.

RIGHT: Returns the specified number of characters from the end of a text string.

MID: Returns the characters from the middle of a text string, given a starting position and length.

The LEFT, RIGHT, and MID functions all work the same way. They take the specified text string and then return a portion of that string based on the number of characters you specify. Let's look at some examples:

	A	B	C	D
1	exactitude			
2		LEFT	RIGHT	MID (start with 3)
3	3	exa	ude	act
4	5	exact	itude	actit
5	7	exactit	ctitude	actitud
6				
7	*Formula In Row 3*	=LEFT($A$1,A3)	=RIGHT($A$1,A3)	=MID($A$1,3,A3)

What you see in this table is that I had Excel take the word "exactitude" and then use the LEFT, RIGHT, and MID functions to pull a specified number of characters from that word. Row 3, which you can see the formula for in Row 7, takes 3 characters using each function.

LEFT returned "exa", the first three letters of the word. RIGHT returned "ude" which is the last three letters. And for MID, we get "act" because in order to get a different result from LEFT I used 3 for the start_num input. That told Excel to start with the 3rd letter and then take three letters from there.

A simple example of how to use these functions in practice is when you have text entries with a set structure. For example, social security numbers or drivers' license numbers.

The RIGHT function can, for example, easily be applied to a series of social security numbers to extract the last four digits.

A more complex example is something like we have in Column A in the table below. I was given a list of values where someone added "units" onto the end of each number.

	A	B	C	D	E
1	Original Values	Stripped Result	Formula	Text Length	# Characters
2	100 units	100	=LEFT(A2,(LEN(A2)-LEN(" units")))	9	3
3	2 units	2	=LEFT(A3,(LEN(A3)-LEN(" units")))	7	1
4	2345 units	2345	=LEFT(A4,(LEN(A4)-LEN(" units")))	10	4
5	678 units	678	=LEFT(A5,(LEN(A5)-LEN(" units")))	9	3

I want just the numbers so I can add them together. Unfortunately, the numeric values are of differing lengths so I can't just use LEFT to strip the numbers out. But I can combine the LEN function and the LEFT function to do so.

You can see that result in Column B. The formula I used is in Column C.

Let's look closer at the formula in Row 2:

$$=LEFT(A2,(LEN(A2)-LEN(" units")))$$

When working with multiple functions in a formula and trying to understand what it's doing, I will often strip away the layers starting with the first function I encounter, which in this case is LEFT.

LEFT takes two inputs. One is the text, the other is the number of characters. So this is basically:

$$=LEFT(A2,[X])$$

Where all of that mess there on the end is X, which in this case is surrounded by parens. If I take away LEFT and those parens, I have this remaining:

$$=LEN(A2)-LEN(" units")$$

which works as a standalone formula. Now, let me break that out into two functions that are currently joined by a minus sign:

$$=LEN(A2)$$

and

$$=LEN(" units")$$

The first of those, =LEN(A2) is saying, "Tell me how many characters are in the text in Cell A2." The answer is 9.

I've placed the answer to that question for each row in Column D. The values range from 7 to 10.

The second is saying, "tell me how many characters are there when you take a space and the word units." The answer is 6 for all rows.

Subtract the two and you get the number of characters to use with the LEFT function in order to only return numbers. I've placed that value in Column E for each row.

As you can see, this varies by row. We have numbers with 1 to 4 digits in that first column.

Now if I go back to =LEFT(A2,[X]) and replace everything represented by that X with its result, I get

$$=LEFT(A2,3)$$

for Row 2. And just like that you can see that the formula will extract only the number portion of the text in Column A.

Now. One thing to note here, that result cannot be used for math just yet. The result of the formula is not a number to Excel. It's text.

If I copy and paste special-values the numbers in Column B to a new column, Excel is going to give me an error mark in the top left corner for each of those values telling me I have numbers stored as text. I can fix that by converting the numbers (as discussed in *Intermediate Excel 365*) using the dropdown:

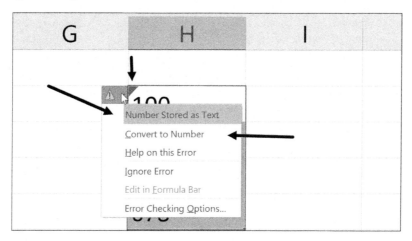

(To save time select all cells you want to convert first so you can convert them all at once.)

Once I do that I'm no longer dealing with text entries. I now have numbers that I can add, divide, multiply, etc. Much easier than manually re-entering the values into a worksheet, especially if there are a lot of them.

If you're working in Japanese, Chinese, or Korean you may need to use alternate versions of these functions, LEFTB, RIGHTB, and MIDB which look at bytes instead of characters.

Now on to the EXACT function, one I don't use but should.

The EXACT Function

Notation:
EXACT(text1, text2)

Excel Definition:
Checks whether two text strings are exactly the same, and returns TRUE or FALSE.
EXACT is case-sensitive.

The EXACT function is a very simple function, one that I never thought to look for because I just used an IF function to do the same thing. Basically, what it does is compares two text strings to see if they are exactly the same.

Here are a few examples:

	A	B	C	D
1	**Text 1**	**Text 2**	**Result**	**Formula**
2	Hey, how are you	Hey, how are you	**TRUE**	=EXACT(A2,B2)
3	Hey, how are you	Hey how are you	**FALSE**	=EXACT(A3,B3)
4	Hey, how are you	Hey, how are you	**FALSE**	=EXACT(A4,B4)

Column A for all three examples is exactly the same, "Hey, how are you". That is also the text used in Cell B2 and you can see that when we use the EXACT function to compare the contents of A2 to B2 that we get a TRUE result from Excel, meaning, yes, they are exactly equal.

In Row 3 I removed the comma from the phrase in Cell B3 so Excel returned a FALSE result because the text in the two cells is no longer exactly the same.

In Row 4 you can't see the difference but what I did is added two spaces at the end of the text in Cell B4. Again no longer exactly the same, so again a FALSE result.

When might you use this?

In the dark ages, so about five years ago, I used to advertise through Amazon but their reports would not tell me my ad performance for a recent time period. All I had were today's results. But I could back into the ad performance for a time period by keeping different versions of that report and then comparing the values in the old one to the new one to see what had changed.

Problem was, the way they listed new advertisements put that data in the midst of my old ads. With a couple hundred ads I didn't want to have to manually go through and compare line-by-line to find where a new ad was shown, but I could put an IF function in place between the two sets of data and immediately find where the ad listed in Row 10 for the old data was not the same as the ad listed in Row 10 for the new data.

The EXACT function would've let me do that same comparison, with a few less steps. (But I'm very fond of IF functions, and their new iteration, IFS.)

There may be other uses. I suspect it was built for behind the scenes use at Excel for functions like VLOOKUP that sometimes look for an exact match. You could also nestle it in an IF or IFS function to trigger the function to do a calculation or return a result only if the text values match between one spot and another.

Anyway. If you need it, that's how it works. Pretty straight-forward. Now on to the TEXT function.

The TEXT Function

Notation:
TEXT(value, format_text)

Excel Definition:
Converts a value to text in a specific number format.

I want to cover the TEXT function now, because it does one thing that I really, really love. But I'm not covering the other aspect of the function which is basically a formatting function, because it can go horribly wrong.

Let's start with what I love and then I'll very, very briefly touch on the other use of the function and point you towards the help text if you want to go down that particular road.

What TEXT can do is take a date value and give you back the day of the week or the month associated with that date. Let's look at a couple of examples:

	A	B	C	D	E	F	G	H	I
1	Sample	d	dd	ddd	dddd	m	mm	mmm	mmmm
2	10/15/2022	15	15	Sat	Saturday	10	10	Oct	October
3	31-Jul-22	31	31	Sun	Sunday	7	07	Jul	July
4									
5	*Formula in Cell B2:*		*=TEXT($A2,B$1)*						

In Cell A2 I've put the date notation for October 15, 2022 and in Cell A3 the date notation for July 31, 2022.

In Row 1, Columns B through I, I've put the various inputs for format_text that I wanted to show you here. Those are d, dd, ddd, and dddd for day of the week and then m, mm, mmm, and mmmm for the month.

In Cells B2 through I3 you can see the results of applying the TEXT function to each of the dates in Column A and using the various format_text choices. I included the d and dd and m and mm ones just for thoroughness, but what I wanted to show you is the ddd and dddd results and the mmm and mmmm results.

(That is a mouthful to say.)

You can see an example of the formula I used in Cell C5:

$$=TEXT(\$A2,B\$1)$$

That is actually the only formula I had to write to build this table. Note that I put a dollar sign (\$) before the A referencing Cell A2 and the 1 referencing Cell B1. What that did was let me take this formula and copy it to the rest of the cells in the table. Excel adjusted the row number for A2 but left the A portion alone and then it adjusted the column letter for B1 but left the row number portion alone.

That means that the final formula, in Cell I3, becomes:

$$=TEXT(\$A3,I\$1)$$

All thanks to the hard work of Excel. A nice trick to learn.

If I hadn't put the format_text portion in a cell like I did here, I'd need to include the format_text input in quotes, so that it knows I'm not referencing some named value. Like this:

$$=TEXT(A2,"d")$$

Okay. The results.

When you use ddd or mmm for the format_text input for the TEXT function and use that with a date, Excel will return a short version of the day of the week for that date or the month for that date, respectively. And when you use dddd and mmmm it spells the day of the week or the month out completely.

In these examples we get Sat and Sun and then Oct and Jul for the short versions. And Saturday and Sunday and then October and July for the long versions.

This little trick that TEXT does has come in handy for me a couple of times over the years, so it's one worth learning.

The other way to use TEXT is something I personally have never had to do. It converts your numeric value to text and formats it based upon how you tell Excel to format the value. I think the use for this is if you're creating a final report and want to generate something like $12.00/unit when you have 12 in a cell.

The help text for this one includes a number of examples and a very large workbook with more examples. All I'll say here is be careful with this one, because it's possible to get number formatting that makes absolutely no sense. Maybe I'm just very good at breaking things, but I covered this in more detail in *50 Useful Excel Functions* and was able to have Excel create formatted numbers where there was a number with a period but then nothing after the period or where there was a weird gap in the middle of the number.

So if you are going to use it for that sort of formatting, I recommend using one of the Excel-provided formats.

Next let's cover some very easy date functions and then we'll start working with more complex functions after that.

The TODAY and NOW Functions

Notation:
TODAY()

NOW()

Excel Definition:
TODAY: Returns the current date formatted as a date.

NOW: Returns the current date and time formatted as a date and time.

The TODAY and NOW functions are very simple functions that work in the exact same way. They have no inputs, so when you use them simply type:

=TODAY()

=NOW()

TODAY will return the current date with an associated time of day of midnight. NOW will return the current date and the current time.

To combine them with another function, like say the TEXT function we just covered, you still need to include those open and closing parens, like so:

=TEXT(NOW(),"ddd")

This formula would return the current day of the week.

TODAY and NOW are dynamic, meaning they continually update the value they return. Since NOW returns not just the current date but also the current time of day it is updating each second although it will only show a new value when you use F9 or open the worksheet or enter a value in another cell and then hit Enter.

So if you're using it and it matters that the value lock in when used, then you need to grab that value immediately and lock that into something that isn't a formula. Or, you can type

=NOW() or =TODAY() into a cell, highlight it, and then use F9. That will immediately do the calculation and replace it with the value.

Now, we haven't talked about this yet, but Excel stores dates behind the scenes as numbers. A date is basically a numeric count from a starting point set by Excel. If you use the F9 trick Excel is going to return the result as that number. I just did it with NOW() and the number it returned for me was 44907.3724212963.

That looks horrible, but you just format as a short date or whatever date/time format you need and it will be fine and once more look like a date. You'll run into this number as date issue often with Excel, so it's good to know about and not panic or get confused when it happens.

The YEAR, MONTH, DAY, HOUR, MINUTE and SECOND Functions

Notation:

YEAR(serial_number)

MONTH(serial_number)

DAY(serial_number)

HOUR(serial_number)

MINUTE(serial_number)

SECOND(serial_number)

Excel Definition:

YEAR: Returns the year of a date, an integer in the range 1900-9999.

MONTH: Returns the month, a number from 1 (January) to 12 (December).

DAY: Returns the day of the month, a number from 1 to 31.

HOUR: Returns the hour as a number from 0 (12:00 A.M.) to 23 (11:00 P.M.).

MINUTE: Returns the minute, a number from 0 to 59.

SECOND: Returns the second, a number from 0 to 59.

The YEAR, MONTH, DAY, HOUR, MINUTE, and SECOND functions all work the exact same way. They look at a date and they extract their portion of that date. The year, the month, etc.

It is important to know that Excel cannot work with dates prior to January 1, 1900. If you format something as a date it must be a date on or after January 1, 1900.

(Note, this may actually not be true for your computer system because Excel uses the date system of your computer to interpret dates and Macs have a different date system. I am only writing about PCs here. Macs use a start date of January 2, 1904. Fortunately, if moving a file between the two systems, Excel adjusts for this behind the scenes, it's just my examples that won't work for you.)

The way Excel was built to handle dates is that each day is 1. And each component of a day is a fraction of that 1. There are 24 hours in a day so .0416667 is equivalent to one hour. And there are sixty minutes in an hour and sixty seconds in a minute so 0.000694444 is the equivalent of a minute and 0.0000115740740740741 is equivalent to a second.

So if I want 1:01 in the morning on January 1, 1900 with 1 second of time added that is the number 1.04237268518519.

Don't try to memorize any of that. Just know that's how Excel works with dates behind the scenes.

Going forward from January 1, 1900 every date gets another 1 added on. So January 2, 1900 at midnight is the same as the number 2. January 3, 1900 is the number 3.

As I type this we're closing in on the 45,000th date since January 1, 1900.

For each of the functions above, you write the function and then include the date or a reference to a cell that contains that date in the parens and Excel will extract that part of that date.

Here are two examples:

	A	B	C
1		12/12/2022	1/31/2021
2	YEAR	2022	2021
3	MONTH	12	1
4	DAY	12	31
5	HOUR	9	0
6	MINUTE	5	0
7	SECOND	42	0
8			
9	*Formula in Row 2*	=YEAR(B1)	=YEAR(C1)

The chart is flipped from what you've been seeing for most of the rest of the examples in this book with the dates that we're evaluating shown across the top row and the functions that were applied in the first column.

For the Column B results, note that even when you can't see a portion of a date, that doesn't mean Excel isn't storing that information in the background. I used the NOW function to create that date at 9:05:42, and all of that information is stored in that date value.

The date in Column C, however, I created by just giving Excel a year, month, and day. Excel created a full date from that, including seconds, but if you don't provide that level of information, Excel will use zeros for the values.

(This is also an important thing to remember when you enter a date like January 1st and don't provide a year. Because Excel has to provide that year. The way it handles dates, it can't sit there with just those two components, it has to fill in those gaps. The default is to set the year to the current year and the day of the month to the first. January 2020 becomes January 1, 2020. Excel can't not do that. Which has caught me out a time or two.)

If all you want to do is see what date Excel has turned your entry into, just click on that cell and it will show in the formula bar. But the functions above let you extract each component and then do something with them if you need to.

More on Dates In Excel

Alright. I'm going to step back for a quick second from listing out individual functions in Excel, because I think this is probably the best place to talk on a more general level about how Excel works with dates.

Above we talked about how Excel views a date as a number where each integer (1, 2, 3, etc.) represents one whole day starting with January 1, 1900 and marching right through to year 9999.

If you try to give it a negative number to get to a date prior to January 1, 1900 that will not work. I get a bunch of pound signs if I try to provide Excel a negative number in a cell formatted for a date. Which means if you want to display a date in Excel that may date prior to January 1, 1900 you'll have to display that date as text (use the single quote in front of the value).

Because Excel treats dates as numbers, addition and subtraction work with dates. I can have a cell with a date in A1 and another with a date in B1 and use =A1-B1 to get the number of days between the two dates.

Just be careful if a date was written with time of day information included, because you may think you're subtracting January 1, 2020 from January 31, 2020 to get 30 days and Excel will return a value of 31 instead because it was actually January 31, 2020 at 12:59:59 PM.

To avoid this issue, either format the result so it shows decimal places or convert those dates to numbers to see this is happening or truncate them to remove any decimal places you don't want.

If you do use addition or subtraction like that with Excel dates, make sure that all of your results fall into the range of January 1, 1900 to December 31, 9999. If you go outside that range, you won't get a result.

Another important thing to note:

I mentioned above that Excel has to fit any date you give it into a number. That includes when you enter 12/15/23. You are not giving Excel enough information there to know whether you meant 2023 (which you probably did) or 1923.

Excel guesses. And it has rules it uses to make that guess.

As of right now, mid-December 2022, the Excel help section states that any date that uses 00 through 29 for the year is interpreted as the years 2000 through 2029. And any date that uses 30 through 99 is interpreted as years 1930 to 1999. (Search for two-digit year to find the help on this topic.)

I expect this to change.

In the meantime, it may become a very big nightmare for some people if it isn't already. Because right now if I enter 12/15/30, chances are I mean 2030. And since dates default to only showing two digits for the year there are likely users out there right now who think they're fine, but have dates that were recorded as December 15, 1930 instead of December 15, 2030.

To avoid this being an issue for you, I strongly encourage you to use all four digits when entering the year for a date.

Thinking it through, because I have no special insight on this, I would think that when you enter a date and Excel assigns that numeric value to that date, that the numeric value is then locked in. So as soon as I type 12/15/2030 that becomes 47832 to Excel and any changes made to how Excel handles dates going forward will not impact the date I already entered. This also means, of course, that if I entered a date as 12/15/30 assuming it was going to be a 2030 date, that it locked in as 11307 and any fix or change or patch that Excel makes in the future won't fix that date.

According to Excel's help you can personally change how Excel interprets two-digit years, but you have to do it for Windows not Excel. It basically works like a slider so each year gets either last century or this one. As you adjust the upper end, the lower end adjusts at the same time.

If dates are really important for how you use Excel and you have a varied population of users who may input dates into your workbooks with just those two digits, I'd probably add restrictions to my input cells to make sure that only 2000's dates are being added.

But also, make a habit of entering a four-digit year or double-checking the year after you enter it in Excel so this doesn't catch you out.

If you want to dive in on this issue deeper, the help topic is "Change the date system, format, or two-digit year interpretation".

Okay. We just covered forty-two pretty easy to use functions, now let's talk about some really useful functions, some of my favorites to be honest, that aren't so easy to use, starting with the various IFS functions.

The COUNTIFS, SUMIFS, AVERAGEIFS, MINIFS, and MAXIFS Functions

Notation:
COUNTIFS(criteria_range1, criteria1, ...)

SUMIFS(sum_range, criteria_range1, criteria1, ...)

AVERAGEIFS(average_range, criteria_range1, criteria1, ...)

MINIFS(min_range, criteria_range1, criteria1, ...)

MAXIFS(max_range, criteria_range1, criteria1, ...)

Excel Definition:
COUNTIFS: Counts the number of cells specified by a given set of conditions or criteria.

SUMIFS: Adds the cells specified by a given set of conditions or criteria.

AVERAGEIFS: Finds average (arithmetic mean) for the cells specified by a given set of conditions or criteria.

MINIFS: Returns the minimum value among cells specified by a given set of conditions or criteria.

MAXIFS: Returns the maximum value among cells specified by a given set of conditions or criteria.

I'm going to discuss all five of these functions together, because they work in the exact same way. The only difference is what calculation they perform, COUNT, SUM, AVERAGE, MIN, or MAX.

What these functions do is allow you to set one or more criteria that must be met before that value is included in the calculation.

If you want a total of all sales for customers in Texas, that's easy enough to do with SUMIFS.

If you want to know the most that a single customer who bought Blue Whatsits paid (where color and product type are tracked separate), you can get that with MAXIFS.

If you want to compare test scores for male and female students of Professors A and B, you can do that with AVERAGEIFS.

For COUNT, SUM, and AVERAGE there is also a singular option function COUNTIF, SUMIF, and AVERAGEIF. I'm not going to cover those here because they overlap the ones we are going to cover and the inputs are entered in a different order so it can confuse matters. But just keep this in mind if you ever find yourself working with someone who has an older version of Excel that doesn't have the multiple-criteria versions available.

For the criteria input, there are a number of options that you can use, including numbers, text, and cell references.

For numbers, you can either write that as the number (22) or use quote marks around the number ("22"). If you want to use a mathematical expression, like greater than, you have to put that in quotes as well (">22").

For cell references, just use the cell reference (A1).

Text needs to be in quotes ("text"). You can also have criteria for text that aren't exact matches using wildcards, but we'll cover those later in this chapter after we've covered the basics.

Here is our data:

	A	B	C	D	E	F
1	**Customer Last**	**Customer State**	**Product**	**Quantity**	**Price**	**Total**
2	Smith	CA	Whatsits	123	$4.50	$553.50
3	Jones	CA	Whatsits	23	$4.50	$103.50
4	Wong	TX	Whatsits	56	$4.50	$252.00
5	Ramirez	TX	Widgets	12	$120.00	$1,440.00
6	McCormick	CA	Widgets	7	$120.00	$840.00
7	Brady	WA	Widgets	8	$120.00	$960.00

We have six customers who live in various states and bought one of two products in varying quantities. I want to answer the following questions:

- How many customers are located in TX?

- How much have customers from TX spent?

- What is the average transaction for a customer from TX?

- What is the most a customer from TX has spent?

- What is the least a customer from TX has spent?

And here we go:

	A	B	C	D	E	F	G	H	I
9					VALUE	TX			
10						Cell Reference (Cell F9)	Formula	Text	Formula
11	How many customers are located In Texas?					?	=COUNTIFS(B2:B7,F9)	2	=COUNTIFS(B2:B7,"TX")
12	How much have customers from Texas spent?					$1,692.00	=SUMIFS(F2:F7,B2:B7,F9)	$1,692.00	=SUMIFS(F2:F7,B2:B7,"TX")
13	What is the average transaction for a customer from TX?					$846.00	=AVERAGEIFS(F2:F7,B2:B7,F9)	$846.00	=AVERAGEIFS(F2:F7,B2:B7,"TX")
14	What is the most a customer from TX has spent?					$1,440.00	=MAXIFS(F2:F7,B2:B7,F9)	$1,440.00	=MAXIFS(F2:F7,B2:B7,"TX")
15	What is the least a customer from TX has spent?					$252.00	=MINIFS(F2:F7,B2:B7,F9)	$252.00	=MINIFS(F2:F7,B2:B7,"TX")

This is a set of calculations performed on data stored in Cells A2 through F7 where Customer State is stored in Cells B2 through B7 and Total Spent is stored in Cells F2 through F7.

I did the same calculation two ways. Column F uses a cell reference (I put TX in Cell F9). The formula used for each row is shown in Column G.

The other approach put TX into the formula by using quote marks around the text. The results for that one are in Column H and the text of the formulas are in Column I.

For the first question, how many customers are located in Texas, we can use COUNTIFS. These are the two formulas:

$$=COUNTIFS(B2:B7,F9)$$

$$=COUNTIFS(B2:B7,"TX")$$

The COUNTIFS function only requires two inputs, the range that has the values and then the criteria. So the criteria here is either the value in F9 or the value "TX". And that first input B2:B7 is the cell range to look at.

So COUNTIFS goes to Cells B2 through B7 and every time there is TX in the cell, counts that cell. In this case, there are two TX customers, so the result is 2.

For the second question, how much have customers in Texas spent, we can use SUMIFS, because we want to sum their spend.

These are the formulas:

$$=SUMIFS(F2:F7,B2:B7,F9)$$

$$=SUMIFS(F2:F7,B2:B7,"TX")$$

Note here that SUMIFS has three required inputs. There's the cell range to perform the calculation on, Cells F2 through F7 in this case. There's the cell range to look at for the criteria, Cells B2 through B7. And then there's the criteria to use, the value in Cell F9 or TX.

SUMIFS does exactly what COUNTIFS did. It goes to Cells B2 through B7 and finds all of the entries that have TX in them. But then it goes over to Column F for the entries that are a match and it pulls that dollar value. Once it has all of the dollar values, it sums them together and returns a total, $1,692.

AVERAGEIFS, MINIFS, and MAXIFS are identical to SUMIFS in terms of the inputs they require and the process they follow. The only difference is what calculation is performed with the numbers that are captured. So AVERAGEIFS takes the AVERAGE. MINIFS takes the MIN. MAXIFS takes the MAX.

Above, I used a different criteria range and calculation range for SUMIFS, AVERAGEIFS, MAXIFS, and MINIFS. But they can work using the same range for both the criteria and calculation. For example, I could look at the total spent for each customer and sum only those values over $250 using:

$$=SUMIFS(F2:F7,F2:F7,">250")$$

See how the sum range and criteria range are both Cells F2 through F7?

Okay, so that was the most basic use of these functions. One single criteria. And we could have actually used SUMIF, AVERAGEIF, and COUNTIF for those questions. (There are no singular versions for MINIFS and MAXIFS, because they're newer than the other functions.) But the power of the IFS part of these functions is that you are not limited to one criteria for your calculation.

Let's expand this now to questions that include multiple criteria. For the questions below, note that product information is in Column C and quantity purchased is in Column D in our data table.

These are the questions we want to answer:

- How many customers bought more than 50 Whatsits?

- How much did those customers spend?

- What was their average transaction size?

- What is the most one of those customers spent?

- What is the least one of those customers spent?

Here we go:

	A	B	C	D	E	F	G	H	I
18						Result		Formula	
19	How many customers bought more than 50 Whatsits?					2		=COUNTIFS(C2:C7,"Whatsits",D2:D7,">50")	
20	How much did those customers spend?					$805.50		=SUMIFS(F2:F7,C2:C7,"Whatsits",D2:D7,">50")	
21	What was their average transaction size?					$402.75		=AVERAGEIFS(F2:F7,C2:C7,"Whatsits",D2:D7,">50")	
22	What is the most one of those customers spent?					$553.50		=MAXIFS(F2:F7,C2:C7,"Whatsits",D2:D7,">50")	
23	What is the least one of those customers spent?					$252.00		=MINIFS(F2:F7,C2:C7,"Whatsits",D2:D7,">50")	

Let's look at the AVERAGEIFS one for this:

$$=AVERAGEIFS(F2:F7,C2:C7,"Whatsits",D2:D7,">50")$$

Same range for the first input, we're still calculating all these values off of the total per customer.

This time, though, our first criteria to apply is in Column C, product type, and we want only transactions for Whatsits. It's a text-based criteria, so we put it in quotes. So far it's pretty much the same as the single-criteria formula examples.

But now we need to add a second criteria using Column D, quantity. To do so, we put a comma and then list our second cell range (D2:D7), and then another comma and list our second criteria that applies to that range (">50").

And so it goes. If you had even more criteria you wanted to apply before you took the average of your values, you'd just add your new criteria range and then the criteria for that range onto the end until you were done adding criteria.

Note that you can mix and match criteria types as much as you want, like I did above with one text-based criteria and one numeric criteria. Have a cell reference for one, text for another, a number for a third, an expression for a fourth. Go wild.

Okay. Now that we have the basics, we need to talk about wildcards for text.

In the examples above, I used "TX". That would only count those entries that had nothing other than TX in the cell. (Or tx in the cell, because it's not case-sensitive.)

Wildcards, however, allow you to make your criteria for text entries fuzzy. (That's my word, not theirs.) Using wildcards, for example, I can write a criteria so that anytime my text is in a cell, Excel will count it, regardless of if there's other text there, too.

The two wildcards are the asterisk (*) and the question mark (?).

An asterisk (*) represents any number of characters or spaces.

So if I use:

$$=COUNTIFS(C2:C7,"*ts")$$

that would count all entries in the table where the product name ends in ts. That asterisk allows for any number of characters or spaces before the "ts" but the word has to end there.

In this case, it would count both Widgets and Whatsits. They are different length words that both end in "ts".

You can use multiple asterisks, too. So if I want to count all products with an e in the name, I could do that with:

$$=COUNTIFS(C2:C7,"*e*")$$

That's saying there can be any number of characters to the left and any number of characters to the right. All I care about is if there is an e somewhere in that word. (It also works for words that either start with or end with an e because that "any number of characters or spaces" can be zero.)

If you want to limit things more than that and only include words of a certain length or only include words where the position of the text matters, then you can use the question mark (?) instead.

The question mark represents one single character or space.

And it does literally represent a single character or space. So if I have TX in a field and I use a search criteria of "?TX", Excel will not count that TX entry because there is not a space or a character before the TX.

Another example:

$$=COUNTIFS(C2:C7,"Widget?")$$

would count "Widgets", because it has one singular character after Widget. But it would not count "Widgets – Blue" because that has more than one character after Widget.

You can use multiple question marks, too. Just remember that each one represents a single character or space.

What about situations where what you want to search for actually includes an asterisk or a question mark? In those cases include a tilde (~) before the mark to tell Excel to treat it as itself and not a wildcard.

Like so:

$$=COUNTIFS(C2:C7,"Widget~?")$$

This would now look to see if any cell contained the text entry, "Widget?"

Some other tips and tricks.

If you want to use an expression, like >50, but the value you want to use is in a cell, like F9, then what you need to do is write that with the expression in quotes and followed by an ampersand (&) and the cell reference. Like this:

$$=COUNTIFS(D2:D7,">"\&B26)$$

This formula will count the number of customers who bought more than fifty of a product where the number 50 is stored in Cell B26.

Also, be sure to test your criteria on edge cases. In this example if I'm looking for "bought more than 50" I'd want to test 49, 50, and 51 to make sure the correct transactions were being captured.

And make sure that if you're using multiple ranges, either for criteria or criteria and calculation, that they are all the same size. If they aren't you'll get a #VALUE! error.

Ranges don't have to be adjacent, but they do have to be the same size. Because behind the scenes, like we saw with SUMPRODUCT, what Excel is actually doing is taking the first value in each criteria range you provide it, determining if the criteria is met for each provided range, and if so taking the first value and setting it aside for the calculation. It then does that with the second and the third and the fourth, etc. until it's done, at which point all of the set aside values are counted, summed, averaged, etc.

Finally, let's discuss some real-world uses of these functions.

I use SUMIFS all the time in my budgeting workbook. I have a calculation of how much I owe for my bills for the month that sums the individual bill amounts but only if I haven't already marked them paid.

I also use SUMIFS in my payment tracking worksheet where I need to sum the amounts I'm owed in different currencies separately and not include any sales where I've already been paid. I have a table with the currency abbreviations and I use a cell reference for the currency value and fix the cell range of what I'm summing using $ signs. That lets me write that formula once and copy it down for all of my currencies. (I then have a conversion rate so I have an approximate idea of how much I'm owed in USD, which is the currency I actually care about.)

And as I mentioned above, if you wanted to look at gender bias or racial bias across different professors, you could set up a data table that looks at the average, max, and min scores for their students. Something like this:

	A	B	C	D	E	F	G	H	I	J	K	L
1	Score	Gender	Professor									
2	67	M	Jones			Smith				Jones		
3	74	M	Jones		AVERAGE	MAX	MIN		AVERAGE	MAX	MIN	
4	89	M	Jones		86.375	92	80	M	78	96	67	
5	70	M	Jones		74	82	70	F	83.8	97	73	
6	72	M	Jones									
7	78	M	Jones		Formula in E4	=AVERAGEIFS($A$2:$A$27,$C$2:$C$27,$E$2,$B$2:$B$27,$H4)						
8	96	M	Jones		Formula in J5	=MAXIFS($A$2:$A$27,$C$2:$C$27,$I$2,$B$2:$B$27,$H5)						
9	89	F	Jones									
10	73	F	Jones									
11	85	F	Jones									
12	97	F	Jones									
13	75	F	Jones									
14	71	F	Smith									
15	78	F	Smith									
16	70	F	Smith									
17	73	F	Smith									
18	70	F	Smith									
19	82	F	Smith									
20	86	M	Smith									
21	86	M	Smith									
22	84	M	Smith									
23	92	M	Smith									
24	89	M	Smith									
25	91	M	Smith									
26	83	M	Smith									
27	80	M	Smith									

In Column A we have a series of test scores for students. In Column B we have the student's gender (I'm just going with M/F here). In Column C we have the Professor.

In Columns E through K and Rows 2 through 4 I have built a table that applies the AVERAGEIFS, MAXIFS, and MINIFS functions to that data based upon the professor and the student gender so that we can easily compare max, min, and average between male and female students for each professor.

I rigged this data so that one of the professors had a clear bias that would show in the results. You can look at the data table and see which one you think it was.

In Rows 7 and 8 I've shared a couple of the formulas I used for this so you can see how you can build a table like this and then fix cell references to make it easier to copy instead of having to redo all your work. Here I could copy down for the male row to the female row without any changes needed, but I did have to change the function that was being used in each column and I did have to change the professor field to complete the right-hand side of the table.

In case you can't see it, here are those two sample functions in the screen shot above:

=AVERAGEIFS($A$2:$A$27,$C$2:$C$27,$E$2,$B$2:$B$27,$H4)

=MAXIFS($A$2:$A$27,$C$2:$C$27,$I$2,$B$2:$B$27,$H5)

It's useful to think about how you can use cell references and tables like this to make your life easier if you're trying to get results across the same data table for multiple values. For example, if I wanted data for each of fifty states, using a table structure like I have above and fixing cell references could save significant time rather than having to change the state value in each formula.

Now that we've covered this set of functions I want to cover the IFS function which is one of my favorite functions.

The IF and IFS Functions

Notation:
IF(logical_test, [value_if_true], [value_if_false])

IFS(logical_test1, value_if_true1,…)

Excel Definition:
IF: Checks whether a condition is met, and returns one value if TRUE, and another value if FALSE.

IFS: Checks whether one or more conditions are met and returns a value corresponding to the first TRUE condition.

The IF function has been around for ages. At its most basic it says, "Look at that cell. IF that cell meets this criteria, THEN return this value, OTHERWISE return that value."

For years I would use "nested IF functions" where instead of the OTHERWISE portion, I'd add another IF function. So it would be, "Look at that cell. IF that cell meets this criteria, THEN return this value, OTHERWISE, IF that cell meets this different criteria, THEN return this other value, OTHERWISE return this third value."

You can nest up to 64 IF functions, which would be insane and probably rife with error. But I would often nest five or six.

The issue with nested IF functions for me was always getting the closing parens in the right place. And if you wrote them from the wrong direction that made it even harder.

But luckily for me and many others, in Excel 2019 they introduced the IFS function, which is built for handling multiple possible outcomes.

The IF function, in my opinion, is still the best choice for binary, either/or situations, and I'll show you why in a moment. But the IFS function is the best choice for situations with three or more possible outcomes.

Either one can be used for all situations we'll look at, and I'll show you that, but it's best if you learn them both.

So. As mentioned above, what these functions do is let you build what I think of as a branching path of outcomes. You start off, and if A is true, you go to the right and get a result. If it's not, you go to the left. On that left-hand path, if B is true, you go to the right and get a result. If it isn't, you go left. And you keep doing this for as many branches as you need.

Maybe a better analogy is that it's like walking down a hallway and opening a door to see if what you're looking for is in that room. Open Door A, if it's there, done, pick up the object on the table. If not, open Door B. If it's there, done. If not, open Door C. You keep going as long as the condition isn't met. Until it is, at which point you get your result, whatever that is.

The result can be a value, like a number or text, as we'll see in our first example, or it can be a calculation as we'll see in one of the more complex examples later.

Basically, these functions are a way to return multiple results using one single function.

Let's just dive in now and look at a few examples and then I'll circle back to putting text to what we're seeing.

I want to start with a basic either/or scenario where we're looking at the day of the week and determining what admissions price to charge, $12.95 for Monday through Friday or $19.95 for Saturday and Sunday:

	A	B	C	D
	Values	Charge	IF Formula	IFS Formula
1				
2	1	$12.95	=IF(A2<6,12.95,19.95)	=IFS(A2<6,12.95,TRUE,19.95)
3	2	$12.95	=IF(A3<6,12.95,19.95)	=IFS(A3<6,12.95,TRUE,19.95)
4	3	$12.95	=IF(A4<6,12.95,19.95)	=IFS(A4<6,12.95,TRUE,19.95)
5	4	$12.95	=IF(A5<6,12.95,19.95)	=IFS(A5<6,12.95,TRUE,19.95)
6	5	$12.95	=IF(A6<6,12.95,19.95)	=IFS(A6<6,12.95,TRUE,19.95)
7	6	$19.95	=IF(A7<6,12.95,19.95)	=IFS(A7<6,12.95,TRUE,19.95)
8	7	$19.95	=IF(A8<6,12.95,19.95)	=IFS(A8<6,12.95,TRUE,19.95)

Column A has our numeric value, 1 through 7, for each day of the week where 1 through 5 are Monday through Friday and 6 and 7 are Saturday and Sunday.

Column B has the results.

Columns C and D have our functions. Column C is the IF function. Column D is the IFS function.

For Row 2, the IF function is:

$$=IF(A2<6,12.95,19.95)$$

And the IFS function is:

$$=IFS(A2<6,12.95,TRUE,19.95)$$

Let's walk through those.

The first "branch" or decision point is asking if the value in Column A is less than 6. (I could have also written that as equal to or less than 5, but I'm dealing with whole numbers and it's easier to just use less than for me.)

If so, the function tells Excel to return the value of 12.95.

That's the first logical test and the first value if true. And it's identical for both of the functions.

$$=IF(A2<6,12.95,$$

$$=IFS(A2<6,12.95,$$

At this point the only difference between the two is the s at the end of if for the IFS function.

Since this is an either/or scenario, the next step is to close the function out.

If the value in that cell *isn't* less than 6, which because we know there are only the seven choices means it's either 6 or 7, we need to tell Excel a different value to return.

With the IF function, we can just list that other value and close the function out, so add:

$$19.95)$$

With the IFS function, because it's built to keep going and going and going, we have to give a second logical test. In this case, because we don't need to go further, that "test" is simply TRUE which essentially means, stop here and return this value. So we add:

$$TRUE,19.95)$$

Once more, here are our final formulas:

$$=IF(A2<6,12.95,19.95)$$

$$=IFS(A2<6,12.95,TRUE,19.95)$$

The difference between the two, for a binary either/or scenario, is that IFS needs to have that TRUE component to work and IF doesn't.

That's why it's easier to use IF for these simple scenarios.

If I wanted to describe the IF function we just wrote in English, I would "read" it this way: IF the value in Cell A2 is less than 6, THEN return 12.95, OTHERWISE return 19.95."

Learning to read IF functions that way makes them easier to write, for me at least. Another trick when they get complex is to draw out the paths you've created.

But for now, let's move on to a more complex scenario where IFS can really shine. Don't be scared when you look at this, we'll walk through it step-by-step.

	A	B	C
1	Spend X or More	Get Percent Discount	
2	$25.00	5%	
3	$75.00	10%	
4	$150.00	20%	
5	$250.00	25%	
6			
7	Customer Spend	Cost After Discount	IFS Formula
8	$12.50	$12.50	=IFS(A8<$A$2,A8,A8<$A$3,A8*(1-$B$2),A8<$A$4,A8*(1-$B$3),A8<$A$5,A8*(1-$B$4),TRUE,A8*(1-$B$5))
9	$25.00	$23.75	=IFS(A9<$A$2,A9,A9<$A$3,A9*(1-$B$2),A9<$A$4,A9*(1-$B$3),A9<$A$5,A9*(1-$B$4),TRUE,A9*(1-$B$5))
10	$40.00	$38.00	=IFS(A10<$A$2,A10,A10<$A$3,A10*(1-$B$2),A10<$A$4,A10*(1-$B$3),A10<$A$5,A10*(1-$B$4),TRUE,A10*(1-$B$5))
11	$75.00	$67.50	=IFS(A11<$A$2,A11,A11<$A$3,A11*(1-$B$2),A11<$A$4,A11*(1-$B$3),A11<$A$5,A11*(1-$B$4),TRUE,A11*(1-$B$5))
12	$100.00	$90.00	=IFS(A12<$A$2,A12,A12<$A$3,A12*(1-$B$2),A12<$A$4,A12*(1-$B$3),A12<$A$5,A12*(1-$B$4),TRUE,A12*(1-$B$5))
13	$150.00	$120.00	=IFS(A13<$A$2,A13,A13<$A$3,A13*(1-$B$2),A13<$A$4,A13*(1-$B$3),A13<$A$5,A13*(1-$B$4),TRUE,A13*(1-$B$5))
14	$200.00	$160.00	=IFS(A14<$A$2,A14,A14<$A$3,A14*(1-$B$2),A14<$A$4,A14*(1-$B$3),A14<$A$5,A14*(1-$B$4),TRUE,A14*(1-$B$5))
15	$250.00	$187.50	=IFS(A15<$A$2,A15,A15<$A$3,A15*(1-$B$2),A15<$A$4,A15*(1-$B$3),A15<$A$5,A15*(1-$B$4),TRUE,A15*(1-$B$5))

(Also, let me note here that this scenario may be better handled with a lookup function, but I've always personally disliked those for reasons that may not be true anymore. Don't worry, we'll cover those next and you can decide for yourself. For now…)

What you see here in Cells A1 through B5 is a discount table. If a customer spends $25 or more they get 5% off. If they hit $75 they get 10% off. If they hit $150 they get 20% off. And if they reach $250 or more, 25% off.

It is important when building one of these, and it's a mistake I make often even to this day, that you know when each threshold is triggered. So here it's "spend $25 or more" but sometimes it will be "spend more than $25". Those two scenarios need to be written differently.

That's why in the table of examples in Rows 7 through 15 I've included values that match each discount level. So I can see myself that the formula I wrote works at $25, $75, etc. the way it's supposed to. In this case, that the discount kicks in.

Let's describe what you're seeing in that table in Rows 7 through 15, and then we'll look at the formula.

Column A is the amount the customer spent. Column B is the result of using the IFS function to calculate how much they owe after any discount is applied. Column C is the IFS function that was used.

And, before I deleted it, there was a Column D where I manually went through each of those customer spend amounts, reviewed the table of discounts, and manually calculated what the discount should be to check my results. That column had things like =A15*.75 which is taking the customer spend mount in Cell A15, $250, and multiplying it by 1 minus the discount percent of 25% which is the same as .75.

Always, with something this complex, check your formula independently. Find another way to do the same calculation and make sure that your formula and that other method provide the same result. Once you've done that, you can copy your formula to 100,000 rows and be comfortable that it's working properly.

Writing this I initially had an error I needed to fix and I've been doing this almost thirty years, so never assume you can skip that quality review step.

Okay. Deep breaths. Let's look at the formula in Cell C8:

$$=IFS(A8<\$A\$2,A8,A8<\$A\$3,A8*(1-\$B\$2),A8<\$A\$4,A8*(1-\$B\$3),A8<\$A\$5,A8*(1-\$B\$4),TRUE,A8*(1-\$B\$5))$$

That's a lot, right? But the beauty of IFS is that you can just chop it starting on the left-hand side and look at each component part. So let's do that. Step one:

$$=IFS(A8<\$A\$2,A8,$$

What that is "saying" is that if the value in Cell A8 (our customer spend amount) is less than the value in Cell A2 (our lowest discount threshold), then just return the value in Cell A8.

There's no discount if we haven't met the first discount tier.

Note here that the A2 is written using dollar signs ($) but the A8 references are not. This is to let me copy the formula to other cells and not have to edit or rewrite it. I want any cell that's in the discount table to be fixed, but all of my customer spend cell references to change.

Also, for me personally, it is easier to go through and do that after I have the whole formula. So I didn't add the dollar signs until the end. But it may be easier for you to do so as you go, because I am probably more prone to miss one the way I do it than someone who adds them as they go.

Next step:

$$A8<\$A\$3,A8*(1-\$B\$2),$$

Here what this is saying is we already know the value in Cell A8 is equal to or greater than the first discount level in Cell A2. (If that weren't true, we wouldn't be here, we'd already have a result.)

So we know the value is $25 or more. Now we need to know if it's $75 or more. That's what the first portion of the formula is saying. If the customer spend (A8) is less than the next discount level of $75 (in Cell A3), then perform this calculation.

The calculation is taking the customer spend (A8) and multiplying it by 100% minus the discount percent for that first discount tier, 5%, which is in Cell B2.

A few things to note here. We've fixed the reference to the discount table again, $A$3 and $B$2. Also, I have combined two steps with that formula. A8 times 1 minus B2 is the same as A8 minus A8 times B2. You could write it either way, it's going to come down to how your mind works.

And it may be simpler to you to build the table so that you pull the discount percent using the IFS function and then do the math of applying that discount away from the IFS function. In that case, this would be:

$$A8<\$A\$3,\$B\$2,$$

123

It would just return the discount percent. And actually that approach follows the "make your assumption visible" rule we discussed at the start. And is less prone to error. Because the error I made when I first wrote this was to forget those parens around 1-$B$2.

But I figured this was also an opportunity to show you that the value Excel returns is not limited to a cell reference. You can have it calculate something for you within the IFS function.

And, finally, the other thing I want to point out here is that the comparison is A8 to A3. We're asking if the value has reached the next discount level. BUT the value we pull is in B2, because we have not reached that next level, so the discount that applies is from Row 2, not Row 3.

This is because of how I structured the discount table and how I'm writing this formula. You could structure either one differently and it would work differently. Always think it through. Ask yourself, *what is this "saying" the way I've written it and so what result does that really mean should be returned here?*

Okay. Step 3 is the same sort of thing again:

$$A8<\$A\$4,A8*(1-\$B\$3),$$

Same with Step 4:

$$A8<\$A\$5,A8*(1-\$B\$4),$$

And then we get to the end where someone has spent $250 or more:

$$TRUE,A8*(1-\$B\$5))$$

We tell Excel TRUE to let it know this is where we stop and the result is the final discount percent in the table. Done.

Phew. That was a lot. But you want to see the IF function we would have had to write for this?

$$=IF(A8<\$A\$2,A8,IF(A8<\$A\$3,A8*(1-\$B\$2),IF(A8<\$A\$4,A8*(1-\$B\$3),IF(A8<\$A\$5,A8*(1-\$B\$4),A8*(1-\$B\$5)))))$$

See all those closing parens at the end? And all those IF functions nested in the middle? And this was the better way to write nested IF functions. There's another way to write them where they don't all close out at the very end, but close out at different points within the formula and it can be a nightmare to track a missing paren.

If you ever find yourself in that sort of situation where you have to see if you properly closed out everything, click into the formula bar for that cell and as you arrow through the formula, Excel will briefly bold both the opening and closing paren that are associated with one another.

The way I structured this one above, by arrowing from the end of the formula, I should see each of those last four parens match up with the beginning of an IF function. If that doesn't happen, chances are I'm missing a closing paren at the end.

It's four closing parens in this scenario because that's the number of IF functions I had to use to write the formula. Here I've bolded each one so you can better see them:

=**IF**(A8<$A$2,A8,**IF**(A8<$A$3,A8*(1-$B$2),**IF**(A8<$A$4,A8*(1-$B$3),**IF**(A8<$A$5,A8*(1-$B$4),A8*(1-$B$5)))))

The other pairs of parens in this formula should be close together. I've tried to bold them below, but it may not show well. Look at (1-$B$2) for an example.

=IF(A8<$A$2,A8,IF(A8<$A$3,A8***(**1-$B$2**)**,IF(A8<$A$4,A8***(**1-$B$3**)**,IF(A8<$A$5,A8***(**1-$B$4**)**,A8***(**1-$B$5**)**))))

You can now forget I ever showed you that, because IFS is the better option. With IFS you can list up to 127 total logical tests and outcomes, but please don't. There are better solutions at that point. There may even be better solutions with our table above. Let's go look at those now.

The XLOOKUP, VLOOKUP, and HLOOKUP Functions

Notation:

XLOOKUP(lookup_value, lookup_array, return_array, [if_not_found], [match_mode], [search_mode])

VLOOKUP(lookup_value, table_array, col_index_num, [range_lookup])

HLOOKUP(lookup_value, table_array, row_index_num, [range_lookup])

Excel Definition:

XLOOKUP: Searches a range or an array for a match and returns the corresponding item from a second range or array. By default, an exact match is used.

VLOOKUP: Looks for a value in the leftmost column of a table, and then returns a value in the same row from a column you specify. By default, the table must be sorted in an ascending order.

HLOOKUP: Looks up a value in the top row of a table or array of values and returns the value in the same column from a row you specify.

I have high hopes for XLOOKUP, but this is the first time I've ever tried to use it, so let's see if it lives up to my imagined hype. (Hint: It does!) Before we get there, though, let's talk about VLOOKUP and HLOOKUP so you can put XLOOKUP into context.

VLOOKUP and HLOOKUP work in the same general way. They look in a range of values (either vertical for VLOOKUP or horizontal for HLOOKUP) and then when they find an exact match, or the closest match if that's the choice you've made, they return that value or a value in a related range of values.

Sounds complex, so let's go back to the example we just used with IF and IFS and use VLOOKUP instead to show you what I'm talking about.

	A	B	C	D
1	**Spend X or More**	**Get Percent Discount**		
2	$0.00	0%		
3	$25.00	5%		
4	$75.00	10%		
5	$150.00	20%		
6	$250.00	25%		
7				
8	**Customer Spend**	**Discount Percent**	**Customer Final Cost**	**VLOOKUP Formula for Column B**
9	$12.50	0%	$12.50	=VLOOKUP(A9,$A$1:$B$6,2,TRUE)
10	$25.00	5%	$23.75	=VLOOKUP(A10,$A$1:$B$6,2,TRUE)
11	$40.00	5%	$38.00	=VLOOKUP(A11,$A$1:$B$6,2,TRUE)
12	$75.00	10%	$67.50	=VLOOKUP(A12,$A$1:$B$6,2,TRUE)
13	$100.00	10%	$90.00	=VLOOKUP(A13,$A$1:$B$6,2,TRUE)
14	$150.00	20%	$120.00	=VLOOKUP(A14,$A$1:$B$6,2,TRUE)
15	$200.00	20%	$160.00	=VLOOKUP(A15,$A$1:$B$6,2,TRUE)
16	$250.00	25%	$187.50	=VLOOKUP(A16,$A$1:$B$6,2,TRUE)

The discount table is structured *almost* perfectly for use with VLOOKUP. What it was missing is that new first row in the table that says $0 and 0%. Without that first row the $12.50 customer purchase generates an error message.

The reason this discount table is structured so well for use with VLOOKUP is because the entries are in order and the amount spent column is the first column in the range.

I tend to hate working with VLOOKUP (although I've come around some) because the places where I want to use it do not include sorted data. Or I want to look a value up in Column E and return a value in Column C and that is not possible with VLOOKUP. So before I can ever use it I have to sort and rearrange my data, which is annoying.

But that's what you have to do.

So. Let's walk through the formula I wrote here and talk about the different components.

$$=VLOOKUP(A9,\$A\$1:\$B\$6,2,TRUE)$$

The first input, lookup_value, is the value you want to look up in your data range. In this case that's the amount that particular customer spent, which in Row 9 is in Cell A9.

The next input is your data table which Excel calls your table array. The first column of this range of cells MUST be the column that contains the values you want to compare to. So if I had an extra column to the left of the cutoffs for each discount, I'd have to leave that out of the table array. Excel with VLOOKUP will always look in the first column that you give for the table array. Always.

The table array you provide also has to include the column that contains the value you want to return. Here I'm asking Excel to take the amount the customer spent, compare it to my discount thresholds (Column A), and then return the discount percent (Column B). So the table array I provide has to include both of those columns. The discount thresholds and the discount percent.

You could technically have a table array that was one column. If I wanted to instead return the threshold amount that applied for that customer spend level, I could write a VLOOKUP function that only had one column for the table array.

But here we have two.

The next input, col_index, is the column number within the table array that contains the value you want to return. To get this number, look at the range you provided Excel in the last input, and then count which column from the start contains the value you want to return. In this instance it's very simple. I have two columns and the value I want back is the one from the second column so I use 2 for that.

The final input, range_lookup, is a TRUE/FALSE value. It's optional, because it will have a value of TRUE by default.

TRUE means look for the closest match. FALSE means look for an exact match. If you use TRUE, your data must be sorted.

In this case, we want the closest match not an exact match, because anything between $25 and $74.99 earns a discount of 5%. It doesn't have to be only $25 or only $75 to earn a discount which is what using an exact match would do.

So I used TRUE. I could have also left it blank and it would have generated the same result. Like this:

$$=VLOOKUP(A9,\$A\$1:\$B\$6,2)$$

(I include it because that makes me think through what I'm doing and make a conscious decision about it.)

It's important to understand what Excel considers the closest match. As I understand it, VLOOKUP (and HLOOKUP) starts with the first value in the first column (or row) of the range and compares that to your value.

If your value is greater than the first value, it keeps going until it finds a value that is greater than the one you're looking up. At that point, it drops back to the last value you passed. So for $12.50 it drops back to the value of $0 in our table. For $40 it drops back to $25.

For $74.99 it would still drop back to $40 even though it's only 1 cent from $75. So "closest" is a bit of a misnomer. It's actually "closest without going over".

But when your data is out of order, it really does weird things. I honestly can't figure out the pattern it follows.

Here I've taken our data table and messed with the order of the values in the table:

	A	B	C	D
1	**Spend X or More**	**Get Percent Discount**		
2	$150.00	20%		**THESE RESULTS ARE WRONG**
3	$0.00	0%		
4	$250.00	25%		
5	$25.00	5%		
6	$75.00	10%		
7				
8	**Customer Spend**	**Discount Percent**	**Customer Final Cost**	**VLOOKUP Formula for Column B**
9	$12.50	0%	$12.50	=VLOOKUP(A9,$A$1:$B$6,2,TRUE)
10	$25.00	5%	$23.75	=VLOOKUP(A10,$A$1:$B$6,2,TRUE)
11	$40.00	5%	$38.00	=VLOOKUP(A11,$A$1:$B$6,2,TRUE)
12	$75.00	10%	$67.50	=VLOOKUP(A12,$A$1:$B$6,2,TRUE)
13	$100.00	10%	$90.00	=VLOOKUP(A13,$A$1:$B$6,2,TRUE)
14	$150.00	10%	$135.00	=VLOOKUP(A14,$A$1:$B$6,2,TRUE)
15	$200.00	10%	$180.00	=VLOOKUP(A15,$A$1:$B$6,2,TRUE)
16	$250.00	10%	$225.00	=VLOOKUP(A16,$A$1:$B$6,2,TRUE)

Nothing else has changed. The formulas are the same. The discount levels are the same. The only change I made was making it so that the discount levels are not in ascending order. And you can see that Excel now pulls in wrong values. Everything from $75 and up returns a discount of 10%, even the rows that are an exact match like $250. And trying to apply logic from either the bottom or the top doesn't work.

Anyway. Be careful on those closest matches that you really understand what it's returning and that your data is sorted.

(Yes, I am going to say that a dozen times because it is so, so important. Sort your data when working with VLOOKUP and HLOOKUP unless you use exact matches.)

Okay. In the example above, the lookup column and the result column were right next to each other, but that doesn't have to be the case. I've had situations where the column I wanted a result from was the fifth, or sixth, or seventh. That is fine to do.

For example, I have an advertising tracker that uses VLOOKUP to bring in the book identifier number, author name, and series name from my Title Master Listing worksheet when I enter a title in Column E. Here's what those formulas look like for a couple of rows of that worksheet:

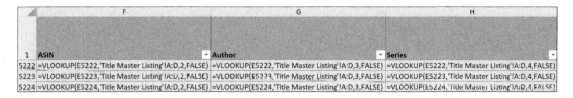

	F	G	H
1	ASIN	Author	Series
5222	=VLOOKUP(E5222,'Title Master Listing'!A:D,2,FALSE)	=VLOOKUP(E5222,'Title Master Listing'!A:D,3,FALSE)	=VLOOKUP(E5222,'Title Master Listing'!A:D,4,FALSE)
5223	=VLOOKUP(E5223,'Title Master Listing'!A:D,2,FALSE)	=VLOOKUP(E5223,'Title Master Listing'!A:D,3,FALSE)	=VLOOKUP(E5223,'Title Master Listing'!A:D,4,FALSE)
5224	=VLOOKUP(E5224,'Title Master Listing'!A:D,2,FALSE)	=VLOOKUP(E5224,'Title Master Listing'!A:D,3,FALSE)	=VLOOKUP(E5224,'Title Master Listing'!A:D,4,FALSE)

The formulas for Row 5222 are:

$$=VLOOKUP(E5222,'Title\ Master\ Listing'!A:D,\mathbf{2},FALSE)$$

$$=VLOOKUP(E5222,'Title\ Master\ Listing'!A:D,\mathbf{3},FALSE)$$

$$=VLOOKUP(E5222,'Title\ Master\ Listing'!A:D,\mathbf{4},FALSE)$$

I have bolded in those formulas above the only difference that exists between them, which is which column to pull a result from.

For each one, it looks at the title in Column E, and the source table it looks in is stored in Columns A through D of the Title Master Listing worksheet. Column A is Title. Column B is Identifier (ASIN). Column C is Author. Column D is Series.

So for ASIN I pull from the second column, for Author I pull from the third column, and for Series I pull from the fourth.

Note here that the last input is FALSE because I only want exact matches. If there isn't an exact match I'll get an error message that lets me know I need to update the table with information for that new title. That also means that my title master listing does not have to be sorted alphabetically, which is nice because that lets me just add new titles to the bottom of the list.

* * *

One more thing to emphasize. Both examples I just showed you have Column A as the lookup column, but that does not have to be the case.

You could have your lookup value in Column E. Or Column AEZ, for that matter. The key with VLOOKUP is that the first column *in the provided range* is the lookup column. So if it's Column E or Column AEZ then everything else has to be to the right of that column.

* * *

HLOOKUP is just like VLOOKUP except it looks for values across the first row in a range and then returns a value from that same column in the row that you specify. Here's an example:

	A	B	C	D	E	F	G	H	I
1			Vendor						
2		Amazon	Kobo	Nook	Google				
3	January	833	171	175	185		Nook		Formula
4	February	998	138	167	230		January	175	=HLOOKUP($G$3,$A$2:$E$8,2,FALSE)
5	March	1,102	221	200	142		February	167	=HLOOKUP($G$3,$A$2:$E$8,3,FALSE)
6	April	1,246	143	171	168				
7	May	941	186	181	250				
8	June	893	238	226	153				

I structured this example so that the data table starts in Row 2 instead of Row 1 so you can see that just like with VLOOKUP the data range doesn't have to be the first row (or column in the case of VLOOKUP).

What we have here is a data table in Columns A through E. Across Row 2, I've listed various vendors that sell my books. In Column A I have different months. And then the table shows (completely made-up) values for units sold in each month at those stores.

I've used HLOOKUP to look for the number of units sold in the Nook store in January and February. Here's the January formula:

$$=HLOOKUP(\$G\$3,\$A\$2:\$E\$8,2,FALSE)$$

Cell G3 contains the store name, Nook, that we want to look up. I've merged and centered that value across Columns G and H, but the value to Excel is stored in G3.

Next is our table range. That's A2 through E8. The first row of the table range needs to be the one that Excel will use to look up the value. In this case, Row 2. We leave out the label in Row 1, Vendor.

After that, for January, it's the second row in the range we provided Excel. It is not Row 2, it is the second row in the range A2:E8.

And then finally, I need an exact match, so I use FALSE. This means my data does not have to be sorted alphabetically left to right.

* * *

Okay. On to XLOOKUP which solves all the issues I have with using VLOOKUP and HLOOKUP. (Before we do this, part of the reason I still covered VLOOKUP in such detail is because people who have used it for years are still going to continue to use it, so you need to understand what they're doing when they do so.)

Let's play with XLOOKUP now and see how they've made our lives easier. I want to work with a new data table that has issues that always trip me up with VLOOKUP and HLOOKUP, so let's put something together that has unsorted values and has what we want to return to the left of what we want to look up.

Here we go, some random book information:

	A	B	C	D	E	F	G
1	Author Name	Title	Related Series	Wordcount	Hours to Write	Genre	
2	Author A	Title A	Series A	26,527	26.5	Non-Fiction	
3	Author B	Title B	Series B	46,204	54.25	Spec Fiction	
4	Author A	Title C	Series C	7,893	6	Non-Fiction	
5	Author B		Series B	6,079	4	Spec Fiction	
6	Author A	Title E	Series C	4,997	4	Non-Fiction	
7	Author A	Title F	Series C	7,976	4.25	Non-Fiction	
8	Author A	Title G	Series C	57,900	23	Non-Fiction	
9	Author A	Title H	Series A	8,284	5.75	Non-Fiction	
10							
11	Lookup Value		For	Result	Formula		
12	Title C		Author	Author A	=XLOOKUP(A12,B2:B9,A2:A9,"Title Not Found",0,1)		
13	Title C		Genre	Non-Fiction	=XLOOKUP(A13,B2:B9,F2:F9,"Title Not Found",0,1)		
14	Title D		Author	Title Not Found	=XLOOKUP(A14,B2:B9,A2:A9,"Title Not Found",0,1)		
15	Title D		Genre	Title Not Found	=XLOOKUP(A15,B2:B9,F2:F9,"Title Not Found",0,1)		

I have put the column with the unique values, Title, second. You can see that the author name (in Column A) and series name (in Column C) repeat, but title values in this data table are unique.

And that's probably something to emphasize here for all of these functions. They're built to retrieve information related to unique entries. The examples Excel uses are things like employee data with an employee ID number. You could likewise use it for customer information where there's a customer ID. Or, as we've done, with numeric values in a discount table.

What you don't want to ever do is try to use it on a table of information where the value you're searching for repeats because the function can only pull one result for you. You'll pull *a* result but not *the* result because there is not a single result to pull.

Like in this table. If I pull title for Author A, there are six potential results. Excel can only return one of those.

So.

Whatever values you are going to look up, in this case, title, need to be unique values in your data table. That doesn't mean you have to have exact matches. We didn't in our discount table, right? But it does mean that for $25 in spend, there should only be one discount to pull.

Okay, putting that digression aside. What do we have here?

Column A is author name, Column B is title, Column C is series name, Column D is wordcount, Column E is hours to write, and Column F is genre. With this particular set of data, the only column I would feel comfortable using as my lookup column is Column B, title. All other columns in this data table could have duplicate values.

That data is in Rows 1 through 9. Starting in Row 11 I have the results of some XLOOKUP formulas applied to that table. Rows 12 and 13 looked for Title C and returned the Author and Genre, respectively. Rows 14 and 15 tried to do the same for Title D, but there is no Title D in the table.

Let's look at the formula used in Row 12:

=XLOOKUP(A12,B2:B9,A2:A9,"Title Not Found",0,1)

It starts the exact same as VLOOKUP and HLOOKUP. What value do we want to look up? In this case, the answer to that is the value in Cell A12, "Title C".

Next, we need to tell Excel where to look. This is different. We are no longer providing a data table for this one. It's just the cells that contain the values we want to look at to see if we can find Title C. In this case that's Cells B2 through B9.

After that we provide a second cell range. That second cell range is where we want to pull the return value from. So, okay, you found my title for me, great, now go to this other range of cells and return the corresponding value for me.

In Row 12 that's returning the Author Name from Column A.

Because XLOOKUP doesn't use a data table like HLOOKUP and VLOOKUP did, you need to be sure that the cell range you provide for where to look and then what to return are the same size.

XLOOKUP also has some fun bells and whistles there at the end. It lets you specify what text to return if there isn't a result. In other words, if it can't find a match to the value in Cell A12. That's important, because I initially misinterpreted it and thought it meant if there wasn't a value to return for author (in this example). But I was wrong.

That text is what you display if XLOOKUP can't find the match to what you asked it to look for. Which means I expect it only matters when you use an exact match.

Those last two inputs tell Excel about the type of match to return and how to look for results.

Match mode is the first of those two. It has four potential choices, 0, -1, 1, and 2.

The default is an exact match. (Yay, unlike VLOOKUP and HLOOKUP.) You can either leave this field blank and just put a comma to move to the next input or you can provide a value of 0, like I did.

If there is no exact match AND you didn't tell it what text to return then it will return a result of #N/A.

The next choice is exact match, but if none is found return the next smallest value. Use a negative one (-1) for that.

Then you have exact match, but if none is found return the next largest value. (Exciting that you have this choice now.) Use a one (1) for that.

And finally you can use a two (2) for a wildcard-type match that uses the * and ? that we discussed with COUNTIFS.

After match mode you can specify a search mode.

The default for that is to start with the first item, so you can leave it blank if you want. Or you can use a one like I did in the example above.

A negative one (-1) will search from the last item.

A two (2) is what to use when the data is sorted in ascending order.

A negative two (-2) is what to use when the data is sorted in descending order.

So much more control! This is very exciting. I know you aren't feeling it the way I am, but it is.

Let's circle back to our earlier examples that used VLOOKUP and HLOOKUP and let's replace those with XLOOKUP.

Here's our first VLOOKUP discount table example, but with XLOOKUP instead:

	A	B	C	D
1	Spend X or More	Get Percent Discount		
2	$0.00	0%		
3	$25.00	5%		
4	$75.00	10%		
5	$150.00	20%		
6	$250.00	25%		
7				
8	Customer Spend	Discount Percent	Customer Final Cost	XLOOKUP Formula for Column B
9	$12.50	0%	$12.50	=XLOOKUP(A9,$A$2:$A$6,$B$2:$B$6,,-1,2)
10	$25.00	5%	$23.75	=XLOOKUP(A10,$A$2:$A$6,$B$2:$B$6,,-1,2)
11	$40.00	5%	$38.00	=XLOOKUP(A11,$A$2:$A$6,$B$2:$B$6,,-1,2)
12	$75.00	10%	$67.50	=XLOOKUP(A12,$A$2:$A$6,$B$2:$B$6,,-1,2)
13	$100.00	10%	$90.00	=XLOOKUP(A13,$A$2:$A$6,$B$2:$B$6,,-1,2)
14	$150.00	20%	$120.00	=XLOOKUP(A14,$A$2:$A$6,$B$2:$B$6,,-1,2)
15	$200.00	20%	$160.00	=XLOOKUP(A15,$A$2:$A$6,$B$2:$B$6,,-1,2)
16	$250.00	25%	$187.50	=XLOOKUP(A16,$A$2:$A$6,$B$2:$B$6,,-1,2)

The formula for the value in Cell A9 is now:

$$=XLOOKUP(A9,\$A\$2:\$A\$6,\$B\$2:\$B\$6,,-1,2)$$

That says, look for the value in Cell A9 in the range of cells between A2 and A6. Return the value in B2 through B6. Don't return text if there's no match. (That's the nothing between those commas there.)

And then I used -1 for the match mode, which drops down to the lower discount level when there's no exact match and a number is between two values. (So $40 goes to $25 not $75.)

And 2 for the search mode to say that my data table was sorted in ascending order.

And it works! Woohoo. I really like XLOOKUP. Thank you Excel folks.

Next. Let's look at the unsorted discount table that didn't work with VLOOKUP.

	A	B	C	D
1	Spend X or More	Get Percent Discount		
2	$150.00	20%		
3	$0.00	0%		
4	$250.00	25%		
5	$25.00	5%		
6	$75.00	10%		
7				
8	Customer Spend	Discount Percent	Customer Final Cost	XLOOKUP Formula for Column B
9	$12.50	0%	$12.50	=XLOOKUP(A9,$A$2:$A$6,$B$2:$B$6,,-1,1)
10	$25.00	5%	$23.75	=XLOOKUP(A10,$A$2:$A$6,$B$2:$B$6,,-1,1)
11	$40.00	5%	$38.00	=XLOOKUP(A11,$A$2:$A$6,$B$2:$B$6,,-1,1)
12	$75.00	10%	$67.50	=XLOOKUP(A12,$A$2:$A$6,$B$2:$B$6,,-1,1)
13	$100.00	10%	$90.00	=XLOOKUP(A13,$A$2:$A$6,$B$2:$B$6,,-1,1)
14	$150.00	20%	$120.00	=XLOOKUP(A14,$A$2:$A$6,$B$2:$B$6,,-1,1)
15	$200.00	20%	$160.00	=XLOOKUP(A15,$A$2:$A$6,$B$2:$B$6,,-1,1)
16	$250.00	25%	$187.50	=XLOOKUP(A16,$A$2:$A$6,$B$2:$B$6,,-1,1)

And there it is. It works! (I may send a marriage proposal to whoever did the work on XLOOKUP. I'm serious. Not in a creepy way, but in a "thank you for removing the things that create so many user errors when people try to use VLOOKUP." This is one of those improvements that someone made to a long-running software program that has huge benefits for users which are quite frankly somewhat rare after a certain stage. But the COUNTIFS, SUMIFS, etc. changes a few releases back and this one are spot on, absolutely worth having the latest edition of the software sort of changes. Give those people some bonuses.)

Okay, enough gushing.

Here's the formula for Cell A9:

$$=XLOOKUP(A9,\$A\$2:\$A\$6,\$B\$2:\$B\$6,,-1,1)$$

The beginning of the formula is the exact same as last time. What's different is the final input. I used 1 here instead of 2, because the data is not sorted. Excel, behind the scenes, sorted the values and then looked through for the proper discount percents.

And it worked!

One last example. Our HLOOKUP example. Because I need to show you that this can work horizontally, too.

▲	A	B	C	D	E	F	G	H	I
1		Vendor							
2		Amazon	Kobo	Nook	Google				
3	January	833	171	175	185		Nook		Formula
4	February	998	130	167	230		January	175	=XLOOKUP(G3,B2:E2,B3:E3,,0,1)
5	March	1,102	221	200	142		February	167	=XLOOKUP(G3,B2:E2,B4:E4,,0,1)
6	April	1,246	143	171	168				
7	May	941	186	181	250				
8	June	893	238	226	153				

Here we are. Same data table we used for HLOOKUP, but now we have this formula for February:

$$=XLOOKUP(G3,B2:E2,B4:E4,,0,1)$$

First input, same as any of the examples, is the value we want to look for, in this case Nook that's in Cell G3.

Second input, where to look, is a range of cells across a row this time instead of down a column. That's Cells B2 through E2.

Third input is where to pull a result from. This is also a range of cells across a row. And just like with our columns, the size of the cell range needs to match the range we provided for where to look. So that's Cells B4 through E4.

I don't need it to return text if there's no match so I left it blank, that's the next comma.

And then I said Exact Match (0) and search first to last (1).

Since exact match and search first to last are the defaults and I'm okay returning #N/A if there's no match, I could also write that as:

$$=XLOOKUP(G3,B2:E2,B3:E3)$$

You can leave off those optional inputs at the end if you want to go with the default.

Okay. So that was VLOOKUP, HLOOKUP, and XLOOKUP. I think it was important to teach you VLOOKUP because it was a very, very popular function for many, many years so if you're going to work with other people who have been using Excel for a while it is almost a certainty that they will use VLOOKUP if they're programming sorts.

Also, there's that backwards compatibility issue. XLOOKUP has only just been widely released so most users with on-premise versions of Excel or older worksheets will still be using VLOOKUP and HLOOKUP.

But for a new user, if you don't have to worry about playing well with others, just go straight to XLOOKUP. It does everything VLOOKUP and HLOOKUP can do, but better. Beautiful.

Okay. Stop here if you just wanted the basics. There are a few more things you can do with XLOOKUP that I want to cover, but they may also be more than an average user wants to know. So if you're that average user, no worries, carry on and move to the next chapter.

But if you want to keep going…Here we go.

XLOOKUP can actually return multiple results. Remember my example above where I have a tracking worksheet that takes my title and then looks up an identifier, author name, and series name? And how that required three separate VLOOKUP functions?

We can use XLOOKUP to return all three at once. The formula becomes:

=XLOOKUP(E5222,'Title Master Listing'!A:A,'Title Master Listing'!B:D)

That works as long as the columns where I want those values returned match the order of those values in my Title Master Listing worksheet.

So what did I change here to make it do that? How does this work?

The first input is unchanged. What cell has the lookup value? E5222

The second input is also unchanged. What range should we look for title in? Column A in the Title Master Listing worksheet.

It's the third one that pulls the multiple values. Instead of putting 'Title Master Listing'!B:B so that Excel pulls the result from one column, we now have 'Title Master Listing'!B:**D** which is Columns B, C, and D. So Excel pulls the values across all three of those columns as its result.

Pretty cool, huh?

Because Excel returns results across columns (or rows) when you do this, you need to be deliberate about doing so because you need to make sure that the order between the lookup table and where you're placing those results match. You may also occasionally run into a #SPILL! error if there aren't enough blank cells available to display all of the returned values.

Another weird thing that XLOOKUP can do is it can actually look up two values and return all of the results in between. Here's a simple data table with total units sold per month for a year. (Randomly generated data using RANDBETWEEN for each quarter.)

	A	B	C	D	E	F	G
1		Units Sold		Start	End	Total	Formula
2	January	1,253		January	March	4076	=SUM(XLOOKUP(D2,$A$2:$A$13,$B$2:$B$13):XLOOKUP(E2,$A$2:$A$13,$B$2:$B$13))
3	February	1,417		April	June	2744	=SUM(XLOOKUP(D3,$A$2:$A$13,$B$2:$B$13):XLOOKUP(E3,$A$2:$A$13,$B$2:$B$13))
4	March	1,406		July	September	2106	=SUM(XLOOKUP(D4,$A$2:$A$13,$B$2:$B$13):XLOOKUP(E4,$A$2:$A$13,$B$2:$B$13))
5	April	929		October	December	3142	=SUM(XLOOKUP(D5,$A$2:$A$13,$B$2:$B$13):XLOOKUP(E5,$A$2:$A$13,$B$2:$B$13))
6	May	850					
7	June	965					
8	July	736					
9	August	660					
10	September	710					
11	October	1,041					
12	November	942					
13	December	1,159					

Column A is the month. Column B is the units. In Columns D and E I have months that set each quarterly range. So quarter one is January to March, quarter two is April to June, etc.

Column F is the calculation. Column G shows the formula used in Column F.

Here is the formula for the first quarter:

=SUM(XLOOKUP(D2,$A$2:$A$13,$B$2:$B$13):XLOOKUP(E2,$A$2:$A$13,$B$2:$B$13))

That looks complex, but it's basically the SUM function wrapped around two XLOOKUP functions that are separated with a colon (:) which is used to join the two ends of a cell range.

Let's pull out the first XLOOKUP function in the formula:

XLOOKUP(D2,$A$2:$A$13,$B$2:$B13)

That says, look up the value in Cell D2 (January) in the range A2 through A13 and return the corresponding value in the range B2 through B13.

But here's where it gets weird. Behind the scenes, because it's the SUM function and we use the colon to separate the two uses of the XLOOKUP function, what we actually get is the cell reference for that result. It returns B2 in this case.

Same happens for the other XLOOKUP function. It returns B4.

And what we end up with is

=SUM(B2:B4)

which in this case is 4,076 for that first quarter.

I just tested this with the AVERAGE, COUNT, MIN, MAX, and PRODUCT functions as well and it still worked for each of them. So basically you can use XLOOKUP with other Excel functions where XLOOKUP sets the cell range to use in the function.

I haven't thought through all the implications of that yet, but I'd think that's pretty powerful. The reason I put it here in the "know more" portion of the chapter is because it's very counterintuitive to me that it works that way. I wouldn't expect it to return a cell reference, I'd expect it to return the value from that cell, so it's a little twisty to me how it works. But it does. So there you have it.

One more twisty example and then we really are going to be done with XLOOKUP. Here you go:

	A	B	C	D	E	F	G	H
1				Vendor				
2		Amazon	Kobo	Nook	Google			
3	January	833	171	175	185			
4	February	998	138	167	230			
5	March	1,102	221	200	142			
6	April	1,246	143	171	168			
7	May	941	186	181	250			
8	June	893	238	226	153			
9								
10								
11	Vendor	January	March	May				
12	Amazon	833	1102	941				
13	Kobo	171	221	186				
14								
15	Formula in B12	=XLOOKUP(B$11,$A$3:$A$8,XLOOKUP($A12,$B$2:$E$2,$B$3:$E$8))						

What we have here is a data table in Cells A1 through E8. There are four vendors and six months of results. Starting in Row 11 I have another table that lists two of those vendors in Cells A12 and A13 and asks for values for those two vendors for three different months, January, March, and May. That table uses XLOOKUP to populate the values in the table.

The formula you can see in Row 15 is the same as the one used in Cell B12:

=XLOOKUP(B$11,$A$3:$A$8,XLOOKUP($A12,$B$2:$E$2,$B$3:$E$8))

This is a nested XLOOKUP formula that pulls in values when you feed it both the month and the vendor to look for. And it does so even though the source table has vendor across the top and month down the side and the data table to populate has those reversed.

You may be asking how on earth does it do that? Because it certainly wasn't obvious to me trying to "read" the formula.

A trick to see what's happening at each step for a formula is to click on that cell and then go to the Formula Auditing section of the Formulas tab and click on Evaluate Formula. This opens a dialogue box that lets you go through the formula step-by-step.

It's not entirely obvious even then, but what it looks like it does is this:

It replaces B11 and A12 with their text values first.

=XLOOKUP('January',$A$3:$A$8,XLOOKUP('Amazon',$B$2:$E$2,$B$3:$E$8))

After that it collapses down XLOOKUP('Amazon',$B$2:$E$2,$B$3:$E$8) to its column range result, Column B. So you get this:

=XLOOKUP('January',$A$3:$A$8,$B$3:$B$8))

From there it works just like a normal XLOOKUP function.

I would not have guessed that would be the next step it takes, but it is. This is a powerful and relatively simple use of XLOOKUP that can potentially replace a lookup I've seen that combines the INDEX and MATCH functions, but I think it's going to be one of those tools that's only accessible to more advanced users or those whose minds naturally twist in the right direction.

This is one of those times when Excel's help text is very useful. I was able to create the example above by looking at what they did with a table of corporate results for four quarters and then adapting it to my table. Never be scared to copy someone else's work in Excel. (Or if you ever get into programming.) You have to figure out which part is which and how they all work together, but if you can do that it's a lot easier than trying to start from scratch a lot of times with the more complex uses of functions.

So if you really want to get into this, type XLOOKUP and your opening paren and then click on that XLOOKUP in the box below the cell and read that whole long help article and try to come up with new scenarios for each of their examples and then try them out to test your understanding.

Okay. On to something maybe a little easier, but also very useful, TEXTJOIN. Actually, first I want to cover TRIM which is a simple function, but very useful when you need it.

The TRIM Function

Notation:
TRIM(text)

Excel Definition:
Removes all spaces from a text string except for single spaces between words.

TRIM is a very simple but very useful function. It does just what that description says. It takes a string of text and removes any spaces except for single spaces between words.

I've had situations in the past where I imported data from another source and there were odd extra spaces either before or after the text in a cell. So maybe a space and then the text or the text and then an extra space. Applying TRIM to those entries quickly solved my issue.

Also, the reason I'm covering it now, is because when you use a function like TEXTJOIN or CONCATENATE or CONCAT it can be useful to wrap the TRIM function around that so that if, for example, you are joining first, middle, and last name fields and someone doesn't have a middle name you don't end up with an extra space between the first and last names.

That's probably the most useful time to include the TRIM function. I'll show you that in the next chapter.

Both of the following are valid uses of TRIM:

=TRIM(B2)

=TRIM("Mike Smith")

It can only have one input, but as you'll see in a minute, you can combine it with other functions to get around that particular issue.

Also, keep in mind that TRIM is still a formula. So you'll use it and that field will show "Mike Smith", for example, without the quotes, but underneath it's a formula. So if you used a cell reference, like that first example there that references Cell B2, deleting Cell B2 will convert that text into a #REF! error.

Usually with this one, I want to work with the end result, so I use TRIM and CONCATENATE to get my result and then I copy and paste special-values to fix in the result so that I'm just left with the text and not the formula.

One final note, TRIM was not designed to work with a certain type of space that you can sometimes find in text pulled from the internet. So if you have text and it isn't working on that text, this could be the cause. If that happens, see the Excel help topic "top ten ways to clean your data".

The TEXTJOIN, CONCATENATE, and CONCAT Functions

Notation:
TEXTJOIN(delimiter, ignore_empty, text1, …)

CONCATENATE(text1, [text2],…)

CONCAT(text1,…)

Excel Definition:
TEXTJOIN: Concatenates a list or range of text strings using a delimiter.

CONCATENATE: Joins several text strings into one text string.

CONCAT: Concatenates a list or range of text strings.

The first thing to know is that the CONCAT function is a replacement for the CONCATENATE function. The CONCATENATE function exists for backwards compatibility with older versions of Excel, but if you choose to use one or the other going forward and backwards compatibility isn't a concern, you should probably use CONCAT.

The TEXTJOIN function was introduced in Excel 2019 and it does more than CONCAT and CONCATENATE, so that's the one I now use.

At their core, all three of these functions take text in multiple cells or multiple entries and combine them.

With TEXTJOIN you can tell it how to join the separate entries by specifying a delimiter. A delimiter is a space, a comma, etc. With CONCATENATE you can also add spaces or commas, etc. but you have to do so within the function and between each value that feeds into the formula.

Let me just show you. That's probably the easiest way to understand how these work.

⏷	A	B	C	D	E	F	G	H
1		Anna	Jennifer	Jones				
2								
3	Function Used	Result			Formula		,	Comma Space
4	TEXTJOIN with spaces	Anna Jennifer Jones			=TEXTJOIN(" ",FALSE,B1,C1,D1)			Space
5	CONCATENATE with spaces	Anna Jennifer Jones			=CONCATENATE(B1," ",C1," ",D1)			
6	CONCAT with spaces	Anna Jennifer Jones			=CONCAT(B1," ",C1," ",D1)			
7								
8	TEXTJOIN with comma and space	Jones, Anna Jennifer			=TEXTJOIN(G3:G4,TRUE,D1,B1,C1)			
9	CONCATENATE with comma and space	Jones, Anna Jennifer			=CONCATENATE(D1,", ",B1," ",C1)			
10	CONCAT with comma and space	Jones, Anna Jennifer			=CONCAT(D1,", ",B1," ",C1)			

Here we have in Row 1, Cells B1, C1, and D1, three text values, Anna, Jennifer, and Jones. And what I am doing in Column B is joining those three separate entries to create first Anna Jennifer Jones and then Jones, Anna Jennifer.

Rows 4 through 6 create Anna Jennifer Jones with each of the functions. CONCATENATE and CONCAT are identical, so I'm just pulling in TEXTJOIN and CONCAT here.

$$=TEXTJOIN(" ",FALSE,B1,C1,D1)$$

$$=CONCAT(B1," ",C1," ",D1)$$

Let's start with CONCAT because it's the most straightforward. My first input is the first text string I want, Anna, which is stored in Cell B1.

The second input is the space between the first and middle names, which is written as " ". The quotes on each side of the space tell Excel there is text here and Excel uses whatever you place between the two quote marks, in this case a single space.

Next, we list the middle name cell reference, C1, and then another space, and then the last name cell reference, D1.

So with CONCAT or CONCATENATE, you simply walk through what you want to build and list each element, either the cell reference or text you want, separating each of your items with a comma. Simple as that.

The hardest thing about using them is to get the non-cell-reference section written properly. Especially with an example like the next one we'll walk through that includes a comma.

But first let's look at TEXTJOIN. The first input there is the delimiter, which is a fancy way of saying what you want to put between your text values. In this case it's that same " " which tells Excel we want a space.

Next, there is a choice to make, which doesn't matter in this example. You can either tell Excel to include empty spaces or to exclude them. We'll walk through the impact that choice has in a minute. I put FALSE here, but I could have as easily put TRUE.

Finally, we list out the cells with text in them in the order we want them, separating each cell reference with a comma. Since my cells are in order, B1, C1, D1 I just tried:

$$=TEXTJOIN(" ",FALSE,B1:D1)$$

and that worked. So you can use a cell reference range for that last input if it works with your data.

Simple enough example. Now let's look at Rows 8 through 10. In Rows 8 through 10 it's a little trickier because I want different delimiters between my text entries. I want a comma and a space for the first one and I want a space for the second.

Here are the TEXTJOIN and CONCAT formulas for that:

=TEXTJOIN(G3:G4,TRUE,D1,B1,C1)

=CONCAT(D1,", ",B1," ",C1)

CONCAT really doesn't change all that much from what we just did. The second item in the list is now ", ", but that's really it. Instead of a space between the quotes we now have a comma and a space. Done.

(And obviously I changed the order of which cell is referenced first.)

Looking at a CONCAT or CONCATENATE function that uses commas can be a little difficult. And you have to be careful to get the comma inside the quote marks to make it work properly and display, but it's very step-by-step to combine text entries this way.

TEXTJOIN is a little trickier when you want to use different delimiters, but it can be done.

In the screenshot above, you'll see in Cells G3 and G4 I have put the actual delimiters that I want to use and then for the first input into the TEXTJOIN function, I referenced those cells. For the first delimiter Excel will pull from the first cell in that range. For the second delimiter it will pull from the second cell in the range.

Because it's hard to see the spaces in the screenshot, I've described what I typed into each cell in Column H, a comma and a space, and then a space.

Another option, and it's one I usually forget how to do, is to use curly brackets and list the delimiters within the function itself:

=TEXTJOIN({", "," "},TRUE,D1,B1,C1)

You can usually get a curly bracket on your keyboard by using shift and the same key as a bracket. In Excel this is sometimes the way to list out multiple values for an input, but I don't run across it often enough to remember it.

Be careful with using multiple delimiters in TEXTJOIN because if you have more places that need delimiters than you've listed, Excel will circle back to the first delimiter you provided and walk its way through that list again as many times as it needs to.

After the delimiter section, the formula works just the same as before. TRUE/FALSE which doesn't matter here. And then list the text values or cells with those text values in the order you want them. In this case, I do have to list them individually because they go in the order D1, B1, C1.

Now let's look at when that second input in the TEXTJOIN function matters. Here what I've done is deleted the middle name value, so there's nothing to return for that input.

◢	A	B	C	D	E
1		Anna		Jones	
2					
3	**Function Used**	**Result**			**Formula**
4	**TEXTJOIN ignore extra spaces**	Anna Jones			=TEXTJOIN(" ",TRUE,B1:D1)
5	**TEXTJOIN include extra spaces**	Anna Jones			=TEXTJOIN(" ",FALSE,B1:D1)
6	**TEXTJOIN include spaces with TRIM**	Anna Jones			=TRIM(TEXTJOIN(" ",FALSE,B1:D1))

In Row 4, the second input in the TEXTJOIN function is TRUE. That tells Excel to ignore any empty spaces. And what you get is a perfectly decent result, "Anna Jones".

In Row 5, the second input is FALSE. That tells Excel to go ahead and include every cell whether it's empty or not.

The result of doing that when a cell is in fact empty is that you get an extra delimiter, in this case a space. Remember that what TEXTJOIN is doing is going through and pulling the text from each cell you listed, then placing your delimiter, and then pulling in the next text entry. So when a cell is blank you end up with just the delimiter for that cell, but nothing else.

You can sort of see that in the screenshot. There's more space between Anna and Jones in that row than the row above.

Row 6 uses the TRIM function to fix that issue:

=TRIM(TEXTJOIN(" ",FALSE,B1:D1))

It only works if the delimiter in question is a space, but it pulls out that extra space so that there's only one space between the words Anna and Jones:

Excel generates the result that we see in Row 5 and then goes through that result and pulls out any extra spaces.

Okay, so that's TEXTJOIN, CONCAT, and CONCATENATE and how they work. These are definitely ones I've found useful to know.

The TRUE and FALSE Functions

Notation:
TRUE( )

FALSE( )

Excel Definition:
TRUE: Returns the logical value TRUE.

FALSE: Returns the logical value FALSE.

As far as I know, you'll never need to use the TRUE and FALSE functions on a standalone basis, but some Excel functions have a true or false input or work with a TRUE or FALSE result, and just typing TRUE or FALSE doesn't always work.

I've run into this issue a few times while writing these Excel books. Not so far in this one, but definitely in the Excel 2019 version and the original *50 Useful Excel Functions* book. So if that ever happens to you, try using TRUE() or FALSE() instead.

Also, one practical use I can see for the functions would be with an IF function where you want a percent outcome.

Say I'm looking to determine what percent of the time a customer spends more than $100. I can use TRUE and FALSE as my outcomes with an IF function and then apply the AVERAGEA function to the results to get a % that are over $100.

Here we go:

	A	B	C
1	Customer Spend	Over $100	Formula
2	$ 88.00	FALSE	=IF(A2>100,TRUE(),FALSE())
3	$ 112.00	TRUE	
4	$ 79.00	FALSE	
5	$ 86.00	FALSE	
6	$ 82.00	FALSE	
7	$ 89.00	FALSE	
8	$ 127.00	TRUE	
9	$ 76.00	FALSE	
10	$ 109.00	TRUE	
11	$ 90.00	FALSE	
12			
13		30%	=AVERAGEA(B2:B11)

I have the customer spend amounts in Column A. In Column B I've applied a simple IF function with an outcome of TRUE or FALSE depending on if the amount is over $100. You can see that function for Row 2 in Cell C2:

=IF(A2>100,TRUE(),FALSE())

Note I did over $100 not over or equal to. Always check that. Also, note that for both TRUE and FALSE I have to include opening and closing parens after the function name to actually use each function.

In Cell B13 I've used an AVERAGEA function to get the percentage of the time the answer was TRUE since Excel assigns a value of 1 to TRUE entries and a value of 0 to FALSE entries and AVERAGEA will count all ten values when calculating the average:

=AVERAGEA(B2:B11)

Okay. Now on to AND and OR which are two more that you'll rarely if ever use on their own, but that can come in handy as part of other functions.

The AND and OR Functions

Notation:
AND(logical1, [logical2],…)

OR(logical1, [logical2],…)

Excel Definition:
AND: Checks whether all arguments are TRUE, and returns TRUE if all arguments are TRUE.

OR: Checks whether any of the arguments are TRUE, and returns TRUE or FALSE. Returns FALSE only if all arguments are FALSE.

By themselves these functions don't do much for me. But combined with something like an IF function, they are incredibly useful.

Let's look at a simple example where we're going to calculate how much an ebook sale will earn us on Amazon.

The way Amazon works with ebooks (as of now at least) is that if you price between $2.99 and $9.99 they will pay 70%, but if you go outside that range, so less than $2.99 or more than $9.99, they only pay 35%.

Here I have some book prices and calculations that use IF, AND, and OR.

	A	B	C	D	E	F	G	H	I
1	Value	Between $2.99-$9.99?	Less Than $2.99 OR Greater Than $9.99?		Simple Payout Calculation (Column B)	Simple Payout Calculation (Column C)		Complex Payout Calculation	Complex Payout Calculation
2	$ 16.00	FALSE	TRUE		35%	35%		35%	35%
3	$ 17.00	FALSE	TRUE		35%	35%		35%	35%
4	$ 9.00	TRUE	FALSE		70%	70%		70%	70%
5	$ 22.00	FALSE	TRUE		35%	35%		35%	35%
6	$ 2.99	TRUE	FALSE		70%	70%		70%	70%
7	$ 2.00	FALSE	TRUE		35%	35%		35%	35%
8	$ 7.00	TRUE	FALSE		70%	70%		70%	70%
9	$ 9.99	TRUE	FALSE		70%	70%		70%	70%
10	$ 15.00	FALSE	TRUE		35%	35%		35%	35%
11	$ 20.00	FALSE	TRUE		35%	35%		35%	35%
12									
13	Formula in B2		=AND(A2>=2.99,A2<=9.99)						
14	Formula in C2		=OR(A2<2.99,A2>9.99)						
15	Formula in E2		=IF(B2=TRUE,0.7,0.35)						
16	Formula in F2		=IF(C2=TRUE,0.35,0.7)						
17	Formula in H2		=IF(AND(A2>=2.99,A2<=9.99),0.7,0.35)						
18	Formula in I2		=IF(OR(A2<2.99,A2>9.99),0.35,0.7)						

Column B uses an AND function to calculate whether the book price is inside the magic range of $2.99 to $9.99 that generates a 70% payout. Here is the formula used for Cell B2:

=AND(A2>=2.99,A2<=9.99)

Column C uses an OR function to calculate whether the book price is *outside* of that magic range. Here it is for Cell C2:

=OR(A2<2.99,A2>9.99)

Let's look at those closer for just a moment.

With the AND function, in order to get a TRUE result, both conditions must be met. So the value in Cell A2 must be greater than or equal to (>=) 2.99. It also must be less than or equal to (<=) 9.99. If only one condition is met, the result returned is FALSE.

With the OR function, either one can be met and it returns a TRUE result. If the value in Cell A2 is less than 2.99 or it is greater than 9.99, that's TRUE.

You can see this play out with different values in the table. Column B and C should never return the same result. If they did that would mean I wrote the formulas wrong.

But what we want to know is how much are we going to earn, right?

One way to do that is to take the calculations we've already made in Columns B and C and feed them into an IF function. That's what you see in Columns E and F.

For Column E, which uses the result of the AND formula in Column B, we have:

$$=IF(B2=TRUE,0.7,0.35)$$

For Column F, which uses the result of the OR formula in Column C, we have:

$$=IF(C2=TRUE,0.35,0.7)$$

Note that the second and third inputs are reversed. Because a TRUE result for the value in Column B means a 70% payout but a TRUE result for the value in Column C means a 35% payout. I could've kept those inputs the same if I'd instead changed one or the other to FALSE.

That's the two-step way to do this. But the combine-it-all-into-one-formula approach works, too. You can see that in Columns H and I where I've incorporated either the AND function or the OR function into the IF function itself:

$$=IF(AND(A2>=2.99,A2<=9.99),0.7,0.35)$$

$$=IF(OR(A2<2.99,A2>9.99),0.35,0.7)$$

Let's practice "reading" that first IF function. It basically says, if it's true that the value in Cell A2 is both greater than or equal to 2.99 and less than or equal to 9.99, then return a percentage of 70%. If not, return a percentage of 35%.

That second IF function says, if the value in Cell A2 is less than 2.99 or it is greater than 9.99 then return a value of 35%. If not, return a value of 70%.

I rarely if ever think about the AND and OR functions as returning TRUE or FALSE values. I instead think of them in the way I just "read" them for you. I share that, because it may help in understanding how to use them.

(Or not.)

A few more comments. I used cell references above, which is what I would normally do, but you can also use a text string or a number directly within the function. For text, place the text in quotes. This formula for example looks to see if a transaction was for a customer in Alaska who bought a Widget. If it was, it gives a 50% discount:

$$=IF(AND(A1="Alaska",B1="Widget"),C1*0.5,C1)$$

So that was AND and OR. Definitely learn those if you're going to work with IF functions. Now on to IFNA and IFERROR for suppressing error messages.

The IFNA and IFERROR Functions

Notation:

IFNA(value, value_if_na)

IFERROR(value, value_if_error)

Excel Definition:

IFNA: Returns the value you specify if the expression resolves to #N/A, otherwise returns the result of the expression.

IFERROR: Returns value_if_error if expression is an error and the value of the expression itself otherwise.

Both the IFNA and the IFERROR functions allow you to keep Excel from displaying an error message. I mentioned before that sometimes I'll set up a worksheet with division in it and until the values show in that row it will show with a #DIV/0! error, which can be pretty ugly. To suppress that error message, I could instead wrap IFERROR around the formula in that cell to hide the error message.

Here's an example where we want to take the value in Cell J1 and divide it by the value in Cell P1. If that would generate an error message, writing it this way ensures that the cell just displays as blank:

$$=IFERROR(J1/P1,)$$

Note that I had to include the comma after the calculation I want, but didn't have to include empty quotes to get a blank cell.

If I wanted it to display an error message, I could have included text in quotes as the second input to the function. For example:

$$=IFERROR(J1/P1,"Error")$$

IFERROR works with #N/A, #VALUE!, #REF!, #DIV/0!, #NUM!, #NAME?, or #NULL! It does not work with a #SPILL! error message.

IFNA is more specialized. It works only with the #N/A error message. In the help text in Excel they show this being used, for example, with VLOOKUP for a situation where there is no exact match to return.

The nice thing about IFNA versus IFERROR is that it still does allow you to see other errors, like the #REF! error, which can indicate you've somehow deleted information that was necessary for that function to work.

Finally, you can wrap both functions around array functions as well as normal functions. When they wrap around an array function they will return multiple results just like the original array function would.

The CONVERT Function

Notation:
CONVERT(number, from_unit, to_unit)

Excel Definition:
Converts a number from one measurement system to another.

This is one I honestly don't use much, but I probably would have when I was in school and taking classes on lab science and physics. We had a whole month of converting values from kilograms to grams, etc. (I being the weirdo I am found that sort of fun. It was basically finding the right patterns to match up to get the division to work.)

Anyway. CONVERT lets you take a measurement, like Fahrenheit, and convert it to another measurement, like Celsius. Obviously, this only works for compatible pairs like that.

In the help text for the function you can find a very long list of conversion options using the following categories: weight and mass, distance, time, pressure, force, energy, power, magnetism, temperature, volume (or liquid measure), area, information (bits to bytes), and speed. In addition there is a list of prefixes and binary prefixes that can be prepended to any of the metrics to change the magnitude of the value.

The function itself is very easy to use. The hardest part of using it is knowing what abbreviation to use for your from_unit and to_unit options.

You can find all of the available abbreviations in the Help text dialogue box for the function or you can just start entering your function and look at the options provided when you reach each input field.

For example, when you reach the from_unit option you'll see a dropdown menu of the available measurements and you can just scroll down and double-click on the one you need:

	A	B	C	D	E	F	G	H
1	=convert(40,							
2		(...)"W" - Watt						
3		(...)"T" - Tesla						
4		(...)"ga" - Gauss						
5		(...)"C" - Degree Celsius			number is in Degrees Fahrenheit			
6		(...)"F" - Degree Fahrenheit						
7		(...)"K" - Kelvin						
8		(...)"Rank" - Degree Rankine						
9		(...)"Reau" - Degree Reaumur						
10		(...)"tsp" - Teaspoon						
11		(...)"tbs" - Tablespoon						
12		(...)"oz" - Fluid ounce						
		(...)"cup" - Cup						

Same with when you reach the to_unit portion of the function.

If you do it this way, the to_unit portion will only display the available options that are in the same category as the from_unit option:

	A	B	C	D	E	F	G	H
1	=convert(40,"C",							
2	CONVERT(numb	(...)"C" - Degree Celsius			CONVERT returns a result in Degrees Celsius			
3		(...)"F" - Degree Fahrenheit						
4		(...)"K" - Kelvin						
5		(...)"Rank" - Degree Rankine						
6		(...)"Reau" - Degree Reaumur						
7								

Which is nice because it saves you the potential of having an error due to type mismatch between your from units and to units.

Let's walk through a few straight-forward examples.

I have a number of friends who live overseas and are always talking about how hot it is there, because it's 40 degrees out. Now, being from Colorado you tell me that it's 40 degrees out I'm bundling up before I head outside. This is because my friends are talking about Celsius temperatures and I'm talking about Fahrenheit temperatures.

To find what 40 degrees Celsius is in Fahrenheit temperature, you could use:

$$=CONVERT(40,"C","F")$$

(That's 104 degrees Fahrenheit and, yes, I'd agree that's pretty darned hot.)

For a one-off situation like that I'd probably just type it into my internet browser instead, but if you have to do this for a large range of values, that's when an Excel function like this can be a lifesaver.

It's as simple as that. The first part of the function is the value you need to convert, the next part is its current units, and the final part is the unit of measurement you need to convert to.

The abbreviation for the measurement has to be in quotes and is case-sensitive.

Make sure your units to and from are in the same category or you'll get a #N/A error. Same with if you try to use a measurement abbreviation that doesn't exist. This includes if you input the value using the wrong case. So "day" is a valid unit value, but "Day" is not.

Let me add here, too, that even though it's not on the list of available options you can use "km" for kilometers. Also, "mi" is the miles option you want if you're just trying to convert a good old standard mile to a different distance measurement. (The Help text refers to "mi" as a statute mile.)

Also, in the Help dialogue box they show how to handle squared units by doubling the CONVERT function. So to convert 100 square feet into square meters they say to use:

=CONVERT(CONVERT(100,"ft","m"),"ft","m")

By nesting the two CONVERT functions that way it appears to work to convert a squared unit to a squared unit.

(I tested it with squared inches to squared feet and it worked on that as well, I'm just using hedging language here because I haven't personally thought through why that works the way it does. I'm sure someone more mathematically inclined than I am could write up a little mathematical proof to show me why that works that way, but suffice it to say it does.)

Okay. On to another simple function, NA.

The NA Function

Notation:
NA( )

Excel Definition:
Returns the error value #N/A (value not available).

You can use the NA function to mark empty cells. This avoids the issue of inadvertently including empty cells in your calculations.

A friend of mine suggested including it in my functions guides because he had a scenario where he was generating results using an IF function and then graphing those results. When his results generated an empty cell or a null value Excel tried to include those entries in the graph.

He found that using NA fixed that problem, because Excel does not graph #N/A values.

To do this, you could write something like:

$$=IF(A1>10,5,NA( ))$$

In this case, if A1 is greater than 10, Excel returns a value of 5 but otherwise returns a value of #N/A.

Be sure to use the empty parens as I did in the example above or Excel won't recognize it as the NA function.

The INDEX and MATCH Functions

Notation:
INDEX(array,row_num, [column_num])

INDEX(reference, row_num, [column_num], [area_num])

MATCH(lookup_value, lookup_array, [match_type])

Excel Definition:
INDEX: Returns a value or reference of the cell at the intersection of a particular row and column, in a given range.

MATCH: Returns the relative position of an item in an array that matches a specified value in a specified order.

One of the coolest applications of Excel I ever saw used the INDEX and MATCH functions combined together. I don't think that particular use of the functions is within the scope of this book, because it was very advanced (and it wasn't my use so I feel a little iffy in sharing that), but I will cover them here so you have some idea how they work if you want to explore them further.

Let's start with MATCH. What it does is look in a range of cells, either a row or a column that you specify, and return the *position* of a specific value within that range.

You can also have it return the position of the closest value to what you're looking for rather than an exact match.

Note that this is a position (i.e. location) that you're getting back. It will tell you that that value you wanted is in the seventh row of the specified range. Or the third column of the specified range. This is not the same as saying that something is in Row 7 or Column C, because the range that it looks at does not have to start in Cell A1 and what it's giving you is a position within that range.

In and of itself, that's not going to do much for you. But where this becomes incredibly powerful is when you combine the MATCH function with other functions, like the INDEX function.

What the INDEX function does, in one of its iterations, is return a value from a specified column and row within a specified table.

So you use MATCH to find the location and then INDEX to retrieve the result. Let's look at an example:

	A	B	C	D
1	Employee ID	First Name	Last Name	City
2	1234	Joe	Smith	Los Angeles
3	2345	Amy	Jones	Denver
4	1239	Maria	Hernandez	Chicago
5	2765	Han	Lee	New York
6				
7				
8	Employee ID	City	Formula	
9	2345	Denver	=INDEX($A$2:$D$5,MATCH(A9,$A$2:$A$5,0),4)	
10	1239	Chicago	=INDEX($A$2:$D$5,MATCH(A10,$A$2:$A$5,0),4)	

Here I have a data table that shows an employee ID and then that employee's first name, last name, and the city they live in. That's in Cells A1 through D5.

Below that is our lookup table. I want to know the city for Employees 2345 and 1239. Their ID numbers to look up are in Cells A9 and A10, respectively.

The results of those lookup efforts are in Cells B9 and B10. The formulas that were used are in Cells C9 and C10.

Let's look at the one in Cell C9:

=INDEX($A$2:$D$5,MATCH(A9,$A$2:$A$5,0),4)

The first thing to do is to pull out the MATCH function:

MATCH(A9,$A$2:$A$5,0)

That says, look in Cell A9 and then find that value in the range from Cells A2 through A5 and return the relative position of that value in the range. Make it an exact match.

The result of just that portion of the larger formula is 2. Because employee number 2345 is listed in the second position in the range of cells that cover A2 through A5. Note it is not returning a row number. It is returning a relative position in a range.

Which is why when we pair it with the INDEX function, the INDEX function needs to use a similar range. So that the 2nd position for the MATCH function section is the same as the 2nd position for the INDEX function range.

Let's turn back to that INDEX function now and substitute the 2 value for the MATCH function:

=INDEX($A$2:$D$5,2,4)

What this is saying is, look in Cells A2 through D5, go to the 2nd row in that range and the 4th column in that range, and return to me the value that's in that cell.

Again, these are relative positions. It is not going to the 2nd row in the worksheet, it is going to the second row in the specified range. Since I left out the header row, that is in fact the third row in the worksheet.

Now, real quick, when we were talking about XLOOKUP, I mentioned that it could replace uses of INDEX and MATCH. This is a perfect example. Because

=XLOOKUP(A9,$A$2:$A$5,$D$2:$D$5)

gives the same results, but with a lot less hassle.

Still. Let's finish with MATCH and INDEX just in case you do need to use them.

More things to know:

MATCH will look for a numeric value, a text value, or a logical value. It can also work with cell references as you saw above.

There are three match types you can specify. Using a 0 means an exact match. Using a negative 1 means MATCH will find the smallest value that is greater than or equal to the specified lookup_value. Using a positive 1, so just 1, means MATCH will find the largest value that is less than or equal to the lookup_value.

If you use -1 or 1, you need to sort your data or it won't work properly; it will return a value of #N/A. For -1, sort your data in descending order. For 1, sort your data in ascending order.

Excel's default is to treat MATCH as if you've specified 1 as your match type, so be very very careful using MATCH since the default match type requires a specific sort order.

For text, MATCH does not distinguish between upper and lowercase letters.

If there is no match, MATCH will return a result of #N/A.

Also, the INDEX function can return an array of values, not just one specific value. Here is an example:

	A	B	C	D	E
1	Employee ID	First Name	Last Name	City	
2	1234	Joe	Smith	Los Angeles	
3	2345	Amy	Jones	Denver	
4	1239	Maria	Hernandez	Chicago	
5	2765	Han	Lee	New York	
6					
11					
12	Lookup	Result			
13	2345	2345	Amy	Jones	Denver
14	Formula	=INDEX($A$2:$D$5,MATCH(A13,$A$2:$A$5,0),)			
15					
16	Lookup	Result			
17	2345	Amy	Jones	Denver	
18	Formula	=INDEX($A$2:$D$5,MATCH(A17,$A$2:$A$5,0),{2,3,4})			

Same data, but this time in Row 13 I didn't tell INDEX to only return the fourth column. See that the last input is blank. That then gave me everything in my INDEX range, all four columns.

=INDEX($A$2:$D$5,MATCH(A13,$A$2:$A$5,0),)

As you can see in Row 17, I could also write that to specify just a subset of columns to return using curly brackets and then individually listing the columns I want included separated with a comma, like this:

=INDEX($A$2:$D$5,MATCH(A17,$A$2:$A$5,0),{2,3,4})

If you do this, remember that the column numbers you provide need to be the column numbers as they are ordered within the range provided as the first input.

Another thing to know about the INDEX function is that it can actually work with multiple tables. In order to do that, you need to provide all of the table ranges in the first input and then you would need to provide a final input that specifies which of those tables to use. You could create a results table with 1, 2, 3, etc. across the top to facilitate this. (I provided an example in *50 More Excel Functions*, but I'm just mentioning it here. The help function video for this one is excellent if you want to do something like that.)

Okay. On to SWITCH and CHOOSE.

The SWITCH and CHOOSE Functions

Notation:
SWITCH(expression, value1, result 1, [default_or_value2, result2],…)

CHOOSE(index_num, value1, [value2],…)

Excel Definition:
SWITCH: Evaluates an expression against a list of values and returns the result corresponding to the first matching value. If there is no match, an optional default value is returned.

CHOOSE: Chooses a value or action to perform from a list of values, based on an index number.

The SWITCH and CHOOSE functions allow you to return a variety of options.

Excel's help examples for SWITCH are actually better handled with the TEXT function we discussed earlier. They show:

=SWITCH(WEEKDAY(A2),1,"Sunday",2,"Monday",3,"Tuesday","No Match")

But you can do the same thing with:

=TEXT(A2, "dddd")

And with a lot less potential error. It's very possible that behind the scenes the TEXT function when used that way is using a SWITCH function pre-programmed to return those results and they just made it publicly available. Who knows. Obviously the functionality for that specific scenario has been there for a while.

I thought of a couple of other uses for SWITCH, like providing a quiz response:

=SWITCH(A1,100,"Congratulations, that's correct.","Sorry, try again.")

Where Cell A1 is the student answer to a question where the right answer was 100. Or to assign a salesperson to customers based on the first letter in their last name:

=SWITCH(LEFT(A1,1),"a","Jones","b","Smith","c","Carter","Harvey")

Which I'd actually do using a table:

=SWITCH(LEFT(A1,1),G2,H2,G3,H3,G4,H4,H5)

Both of those take the first letter of the text in Cell A1 and then, depending on the value, assign a different salesperson. One just has the letters and salesperson last names in a table that uses Columns G and H.

I'd recommend using the table approach if you ever build something like that because it's easier to change later even if it's incomprehensible looking. (You basically never need to look at it again once it's built if you use a table.)

But…

I think I could also do this easier using XLOOKUP. So it's possible that XLOOKUP has completely leapfrogged any good use of SWITCH. See here:

	A	B	C	D	E	F
1	Customer Name	SWITCH				
2	Smith	Rep 1	=SWITCH(LEFT(A2,1),"S","Rep 1","J","Rep 2","H","Rep 3","L","Rep 4")			
3	Jones	Rep 2				
4	Hernandez	Rep 3				
5	Lee	Rep 4				
6		None Assigned				
7						
8	Customer Name	XLOOKUP			Rep	Letter
9	Smith	Rep 1	=XLOOKUP(LEFT(A9,1),$F$9:$F$12,$E$9:$E$12,"None Assigned")		Rep 1	S
10	Jones	Rep 2			Rep 2	J
11	Hernandez	Rep 3			Rep 3	H
12	Lee	Rep 4			Rep 4	L
13		None Assigned				

Both tables here use the same four customer last names and then one additional entry that's blank. You can see the formulas used in both in Column C. For SWITCH I wrote everything within the function, but I could have used a table there as well. For XLOOKUP I needed that table.

And it turns out:

=SWITCH(LEFT(A2,1),"S","Rep 1","J","Rep 2","H","Rep 3","L","Rep 4")

and

=XLOOKUP(LEFT(A9,1),$F$9:$F$12,$E$9:$E$12,"None Assigned")

where the data on who to assign is in Cells E9 through F12 for the XLOOKUP function, both provide the exact same results.

CHOOSE does something similar. Here's a silly use of it:

=CHOOSE(WEEKDAY(F1),"Sunday is my fun day","Just another manic Monday","Tuesdays are boring","Wednesday, humpday")

Where it basically returns a different phrase for the day based on the day of the week determined using the WEEKDAY function. (Which is discussed in the next section and basically returns a number from 1 to 7 for the day of the week.)

Again, though, I could do that with a lookup function. And that first input for CHOOSE has to be a number, too.

In the help text they show CHOOSE being used with SUM to choose a range of cells to sum based upon that first input value. But again I think I could do the same with an XLOOKUP function.

So know these two exist in case you ever stumble across them in use by someone else, but if you're not intent on learning every single function you can, I'd focus instead on XLOOKUP.

(And, who knows, maybe there is some weird scenario where CHOOSE or SWITCH work better than XLOOKUP and a table of choices, I just cannot think of one of them now.)

Okay, on to a sort of lightning round of functions to close us out.

Fast Thirty-Four Functions

There are many, many, many more functions in Excel, but at some point it comes down to specific needs and what you want is not what anyone else cares about. However, there are functions I've covered in other books because I thought they gave a good feel for what else is possible in Microsoft Excel that I wanted to cover, but in less detail.

That's what this chapter is for. I'm going to cover thirty-four functions very quickly so you know they exist, but not in a level of detail that requires an entire chapter. Here goes:

PI

This function lets you return the value of pi (3.14 etc.) accurate up to 15 digits. Here is an example of it used to calculate the area of a circle where radius is stored in Cell A1:

$$=PI()*(A1\wedge 2)$$

POWER

This function allows you to take any value to any power. You can also do this without a function using the caret (^) symbol. Use decimals for roots. Some examples:

$$=POWER(3,2)$$

is the same as $=3\wedge 2$ or three squared. And

$$=POWER(9,.5)$$

is the same as $=9\wedge .5$ which takes the square root of 9.

SQRT

This function is a specialized version of the POWER function that only takes a square root. So

$$=SQRT(9)$$

would take the square root of 9.

ABS

This function takes the absolute value of a number. So

$$=ABS(A1/A2)$$

is going to divide the value in Cell A1 by the value in Cell A2 and return a positive number even if A1/A2 is negative.

NOT

I only include this function because Excel lists it as a valuable function. It's a counterpart to the AND and OR functions which will return TRUE if all conditions are not met. So you list three conditions and if none of them are met NOT returns a value of TRUE. For me, personally, I can find better ways to write that, including the example they use in the help section that can be rewritten with just the AND function.

TRANSPOSE

The TRANSPOSE function lets you take a series of values in a range of cells and change them from horizontal to vertical or vice versa. It's still linked to the original source, though, so probably the best use of this one is when it's wrapped around an array function to, for example, return the results of MODE.MULT across a row instead of down a column. Like this:

$$=TRANSPOSE(MODE.MULT(B2:B11))$$

SEARCH

SEARCH will tell you the number of the character in a text string at which the text you care about first appears, moving from left to right. You most likely would want to combine this with another function, like LEFT, to extract part of a text string. So if you had 12,500 units in Cell A1, you could use

$$=LEFT(A1,SEARCH("\ units",A1)-1)$$

to pull just the number portion of that entry. It is not case-sensitive, but does work with wildcards like * or ? to pull inexact matches.

FIND

FIND is like SEARCH but it is case-sensitive. It does not work with wildcards.

MOD

The MOD function returns the remainder after a number is divided by another. So

$$=MOD(3653,7)$$

would return a value of 6 because that's how much is left when you take 7 out of 3653 until you run out of groups of 7 to remove.

QUOTIENT

QUOTIENT is the counterpart to MOD. It returns the whole number of times that a number can divide into another. So

$$=QUOTIENT(3653,7)$$

is 521. You can get the original first input value (in this case 3653) by multiplying your QUOTIENT result by the second input (in this case 7) and then adding the MOD result.

LOG

The LOG function returns the log of a number to the base you specify. The default is base-10, but the second input can be any number. So

$$=LOG(32,2)$$

would be 5 because that's how many times you have to multiply 2 times itself to get 32.

EXP

The EXP function returns e raised to the power of a given number. But you can also write

$$=EXP(1)$$

to return e (2.7182) itself.

LOG10

LOG10 is a more specialized version of LOG that is just base-10 but using LOG without the second input is simpler.

LN

The LN function is essentially the LOG function but with a base of e. So

$$=LN(86)$$

is the exact same as =LOG(86,EXP(1)).

WEEKDAY

The WEEKDAY function returns a number for the day of the week for a provided date. The default is to provide a value from 1 to 7 with 1 assigned to Sunday, but there is an optional input to change that.

$$=IF(WEEKDAY(A1,11)<6,24.95,29.95)$$

uses WEEKDAY to assign different prices depending on the day of the week.

WEEKNUM

The WEEKNUM function returns the week number in a year for a given date. By default Excel defines a week as starting on a Sunday and only including dates within that year so there can be a week 53 result. There is an optional input that lets you adjust this.

ISOWEEKNUM

ISOWEEKNUM also returns the week number in a year for a given date, but does so in accordance with the ISO 8601 standard.

DATE

The DATE function is how Excel prefers you to build dates that are used in functions. It takes inputs for year, month, and day and then converts that into the number that represents that day in Excel. But be careful because it will not let you create a date outside of its accepted date range. For example, a year of 1880 is converted to 3780 instead. Also be careful with any negative values because Excel considers 0 a legitimate number when calculating backward from a date.

$$=DATE(YEAR(A1)+5,MONTH(A1),DAY(A1))$$

would create a date that takes the current date in Cell A1 and changes the year of that date to a year five years later.

EDATE

EDATE will take any date and return the date that is X number of months from that date on the same day of the month. The number of months input only works with whole numbers and will truncate any decimal value provided.

$$=EDATE(B1,6)$$

would return the date that is six months in the future on the same day of the month as the date in Cell B1.

EOMONTH

The EOMONTH function is like the EDATE function, but it will provide the last day of that month when it returns the result. If you use a negative value it will go back X months and then provide the last day of that months X months back.

NETWORKDAYS.INTL

NETWORKDAYS.INTL allows you to take a starting date and an ending date and calculate the number of whole workdays between them, excluding any dates that you classify as holidays. It allows you to specify exactly which days are work days and which days are not, so is a better choice to work with than NETWORKDAYS.

$$=NETWORKDAYS.INTL("12/21/2018","1/8/2019",3,\{"12/25/2018","1/1/2019"\})$$

looks for the number of whole workdays between December 21, 2018 and January 8, 2019 with a Monday/Tuesday "weekend" and holidays listed for December 25, 2018 and January 1, 2019.

WORKDAY.INTL

WORKDAY.INTL calculates what date it will be in X workdays. Theoretically it should match NETWORKDAYS.INTL but they treat dates differently because WORKDAY.INTL doesn't count the start date as a workday. It is more flexible than WORKDAY which does the same thing because it allows the user to specify which days of the week are workdays and which are not.

$$=WORKDAY.INTL("1/7/2019",1,"0000101")$$

is asking to give the date one workday from January 7, 2019 when the "off" days for the week are Friday and Sunday.

DAYS

The DAYS function allows you to calculate how many days there are between two separate dates. But note that because of the way that Excel stores dates, you could also just use math. So

$$=DAYS(A2,A1)$$

and =A2-A1 are equivalent.

DAYS360

The DAYS360 function allows you to calculate how many days there are between two separate dates using the assumption that every month has 30 days. You can specify how dates that fall on the 31st are handled using an optional input.

TRUNC

The TRUNC function is a quick way to get a whole number to work with that does not use a rounding method. It simply chops off any part of the number that is a decimal or fractional. So 70.2345 and 70.98123 both become 70. Same if they were negative numbers, they'd just become -70. It has an optional input which will let you specify where to truncate the number. For example,

$$=TRUNC(132798.79867,-3)$$

eturns a value of 132000.

INT

The INT function rounds a value down to the nearest whole number. For negative values it rounds away from zero.

FORECAST.LINEAR

The FORECAST.LINEAR function allows you to predict a future value given a set of inputs. Excel does this by taking a table of known x and y combinations and then using those data points to create the best *linear* fit through the points so that it can predict a y value for any provided x value. In the function you list all of your y values first. This function replaced the FORECAST function, but they do the same thing.

FORECAST.ETS

The FORECAST.ETS function allows you to predict a future value given a set of inputs where the data is seasonal or non-linear by using the AAA version of the Exponential Smoothing (ETS) algorithm. Data must be organized in a specific way for the function to work. See the help text for more detail.

FACT

The FACT function returns the factorial of a number. This is used in calculating permutations. It will truncate any non-whole number you try to use.

$$=FACT(0)$$

returns a value of 1.

COMBIN

The COMBIN function calculates the number of combinations given a population size and sample size without repetition. So, how many teams of three can be formed out of a class of thirty students.

COMBINA

The COMBINA function calculates the number of combinations given a population size and sample size while allowing for repetition. So, if you were awarding three prizes to a class of thirty students and each student could win each prize how many possible combinations would there be.

PV

The PV function returns the present value of a series of future payments. All payments must be the same amount. Be careful to match the rate to the payments. Don't use an annual rate and quarterly payment amounts, for example. It can also be used with a one-time lump sum payment.

NPV

The NPV function returns the net present value of a series of incoming and outgoing amounts that occur on a standard basis (monthly, quarterly, annually, etc.)

SQRTPI

The SQRTPI function returns the square root of a number that has been multiplied by pi. I assume if you need this one, you know why. I cover it more to explain that it is not a default way to take the square root of pi more than anything else, although you could do that with

=SQRTPI(1).

Conclusion

Okay. There we go. By my count we covered 102 specific functions with mentions of a dozen more. Hopefully by now you have an understanding of some key, core Excel functions like SUM that you'll use regularly as well as an appreciation for the breadth of options available to you in Excel. But there are so many more functions to explore.

I'm just not going to do it here because you'd hate me if I made you go through all of them. Plus, there are some of those math ones that are beyond me. I'd have to go learn advanced trig or something just to teach them to you and while I like to learn...I don't like to learn *that* much.

If you get stuck, Esc and Ctrl + Z are two ways to slowly back away from your problem. If you can, hit enter and then Ctrl + Z. If you get stuck in the midst of writing a formula and you just want to start over, Esc often will work to clear that cell for you.

If you write a function and see an error message, refer to the section on error messages and what they mean. Sometimes it's just because your data isn't there yet (like a #DIV/0! error). Often my issue is a missing comma to separate my different elements or a missing closing paren or misplaced one.

Double-click in a cell to see the cells being used in the formula, because that may be your issue if you're referencing the wrong location for your data. I try to start a formula and then click and drag when I can to get my cell references to avoid that being an issue, but it happens.

You've seen a few examples by now of nested functions. Excel can handle a lot of complexity. It really ultimately comes down to your ability to give it the right information in the right order. When working with complex formulas that use multiple functions, break it down step by step. Is this step right? If I replace this step with its result instead, is that next step right? And just keep working through. That's what I do when evaluating nested IF functions, but it works for all formulas with multiple functions or calculations in them.

Don't forget to look at the Excel help, too. They have some excellent help videos on their functions. And if it's a really important project maybe read through the help to be extra sure that you know how that function works. Although, I'll tell ya, sometimes they just don't cover the things I think matter, so it's not foolproof.

Also, if you don't know how to do what you want to do, chances are someone out there has wanted to do the same thing, too. An internet search will likely find you a blog or a video that walks you right through how to do it.

But if you just can't find an answer, then reach out. I will try to find it for you because that's how my brain works. Once I pose a question to it, it must find the answer or be forever annoyed.

Anyway. Hope this helped. Good luck with it. You can do this. Don't be intimidated. Just work with data you can mess up and be sure to double-check your results against data where you know what the outcome should be and you'll be fine.

Index

About the Author

M.L. Humphrey is a former stockbroker with a degree in Economics from Stanford and an MBA from Wharton who has spent close to twenty years as a regulator and consultant in the financial services industry.

You can reach M.L. at mlhumphreywriter@gmail.com or at mlhumphrey.com.

Printed in Great Britain
by Amazon

39456102R00110